Writing
to 14

Geoff Barton

OXFORD
UNIVERSITY PRESS

Great Clarendon Street, Oxford OX2 6DP

Oxford University Press is a department of the University of Oxford. It furthers the University's objective of excellence in research, scholarship, and education by publishing worldwide in

Oxford   New York

Auckland   Cape Town   Dar es Salaam   Hong Kong   Karachi
Kuala Lumpur   Madrid   Melbourne   Mexico City   Nairobi
New Delhi   Shanghai   Taipei   Toronto

With offices in

Argentina   Austria   Brazil   Chile   Czech Republic   France   Greece
Guatemala   Hungary   Italy   Japan   Poland   Portugal   Singapore
South Korea   Switzerland   Thailand   Turkey   Ukraine   Vietnam

Oxford is a registered trade mark of Oxford University Press
in the UK and in certain other countries

British Library Cataloguing in Publication Data

Data available

ISBN 978-0-19-832113-2

10 9 8

Printed in India by Manipal Technologies Limited

Paper used in the production of this book is a natural, recyclable product made from wood grown in sustainable forests. The manufacturing process conforms to environmental regulations of the country of origin.

Cover: Anna Tyukhmeneva/Shutterstock.com.

p8: ZouZou/Shutterstock; **p9:** Steve Debenport/iStockphoto.com; **p10t:** cristi180884/Shutterstock; **p10b:** Nicole Gordine/Shutterstock; **p13:** Stefan Schurr/iStockphoto.com; **p14:** Rodney Keaney/Shutterstock; **p15:** Soul Of Autumn/Vladimir Konovalov/Shutterstock; **p16l:** Eric Gevaert/iStockphoto.com; **p16r:** Andrew Chin/Shutterstock; **p18:** © Bettmann/Corbis; **p20:** Double Photography/Shutterstock; **p24:** Anastasija Kristala/Shutterstock; **p26t:** Sue Smith/Shutterstock; **p26b:** Alex Staroseltsev/Shutterstock; **p29:** Nagy Melinda/Shutterstock; **p31:** Terry Underwood Evans/Shutterstock; **p33:** Monika Lewandowska/Shutterstock; **p34:** Nicole Blade/iStockphoto.com; **p36:** Cuiphoto/Shutterstock; **p39:** Maxx-Studio/Shutterstock; **p40:** chaoss/Shutterstock; **p44:** Ben Heys/Shutterstock; **p47:** Lee Daniels/iStockphoto.com; **p53:** Aaron Amat/Shutterstock; **p54:** Nils Jorgensen/Rex Features; **p57t:** Dwight Nadig/iStockphoto.com; **p57l:** dundanim/Shutterstock; **p57b:** Boyan Dimitrov/Shutterstock; **p58:** musicman/Shutterstock; **p62:** Galyna Andrushko; **p64:** Zinaida/Shutterstock; **p65:** Nejron Photo/Shutterstock; **p67:** Peter Dyer; **p69:** Donna Coleman/iStockphoto.com; **p71:** Sealstep/Shutterstock; **p75:** Peter D/Shutterstock; **p76:** Racheal Grazias/Shutterstock; **p78:** Puffin; **p79:** Philippe Ingels/Shutterstock; **p82:** ACE STOCK LIMITED/Alamy; **p84:** Pictorial Press Ltd/Alamy; **p89:** aodaodaodaod/Shutterstock; **p90 & p91:** Warner Br/Everett/Rex Features; **p93:** Plastilino/Shutterstock; **p96:** Monkey Business Images/Shutterstock; **p99:** Ewa Walicka/Shutterstock; **p100:** Boris Stroujko/Shutterstock; **p102:** © Ira L. Black/Corbis; **p104:** djedzura/Shutterstock; **p106:** wavebreakmedia ltd/Shutterstock; **p108:** Algecireño/Shutterstock; **p111:** Volodymyr Krasyuk/Shutterstock; **p113:** From The Sun history website holdyefrontpage.co.uk; **p115:** John Shepherd/iStockphoto.com; **p116:** Lana Sundman/Alamy/India Picture; **p117r:** NHS; **p117l:** Friends of the Earth; **p118:** KPA/Zuma/Rex Features; **p120:** Horiyan/Shutterstock; **p124:** Adrian Assalve/iStockphoto.com; **p127:** Diana Taliun/Shutterstock; **p129:** Simon Cox/iStockphoto.com; **p131:** Monkey Business Images/Shutterstock; **p132:** Yuri Arcurs/Shutterstock; **p134:** Monkey Business Images/Shutterstock.

Artwork by Giorgio Bacchin and Rory Walker

ACKNOWLEDGEMENTS

The author and publisher are grateful for permission to reprint the following copyright material:

British Library: extract from the 'Voices' project, Mark James recorded1999, reprinted by permission of the British Library.

Geoff Dyer and **P D James:** extracts from '10 rules for writing fiction', *Guardian.co.uk*, 24.2.2010 and *Guardian.co.uk*, 20.2.2010, copyright © Guardian News and Media Ltd 2010, reprinted by permission of GNM Ltd.

William Gibson: opening extract from *Neuromancer* (Ace Books, 1984), reprinted by permission of the Martha Millard Literary Agency.

John Hatcher: extracts from *The Black Death: An Intimate History of the Plague* (Orion, 2008), reprinted by permission of The Orion Publishing Group, London.

C S Lewis: opening extract from *The Voyage of the Dawn Treader* (Collins, 1952), copyright © C S Lewis Pte Ltd 1952, reprinted by permission of The C S Lewis Company Ltd.

William Faulkner: opening extract from *The Sound and the Fury* (Cape 1929), copyright © William Faulkner 1929, reprinted by permission of Curtis Brown Group Ltd, London, on behalf of the Estate of William Faulkner.

Robert Frost: 'Stopping by Woods on a Snowy Evening' from *Collected Poems of Robert Frost* edited by Edward Connery Latham (Jonathan Cape, 1943), reprinted by permission of The Random House Group Ltd.

M Gasecka: 'The Trumpeter' from *The Book of Mini Sagas* (Alan Sutton Publishing, 1988) copyright © Telegraph Media Group Ltd 1988, reprinted by permission of TMG.

Guardian Editorial: 'In praise of...David Beckham', *The Guardian*, 13.8.2010, copyright © Guardian News and Media Ltd 2010, reprinted by permission of GNM Ltd.

Susan Hill: extract from *Small Hand* (Profile Books, 2010), reprinted by permission of Profile Books.

Anthony Horowitz: 'Tips for would-be-writers' from www.anthonyhorowitz.com, copyright © Anthony Horowitz 2006, reprinted by permission of United Agents (www.unitedagents.co.uk) on behalf of Anthony Horowitz.

Rose Macaulay: opening extract from *The Towers of Trebizond* (Collins, 1956/Flamingo 2010), reprinted by permission of Peters Fraser & Dunlop (www.petersfraserdunlop.com) on behalf of the Estate of Rose Macaulay.

Stuart Pinkner: extract from 'David Beckham is Man of the Mash', *The Sun*, 30.12.2011, reprinted by permission of News International Syndication.

Jay Rayner: extract from 'Restaurant Review: 10 Cases', *The Observer*, 11.12.2011, copyright © Guardian News and Media Ltd 2011, reprinted by permission of GNM Ltd.

Jana Seely: 'Dragon Tale' from *The World's Shortest Stories* edited by Steve Moss (Running Press, 1995), copyright © Perseus Books Group 1995, reprinted by permission of the Perseus Books Group via Copyright Clearance Agency.

Dylan Thomas: extract from *A Child's Christmas in Wales* (New Directions, 1954/ Orion Children's Books 2005), reprinted by permission of David Higham Associates.

Although we have made every effort to trace and contact all copyright holders before publication this has not been possible in all cases. If notified, the publisher will rectify any errors or omissions at the earliest opportunity.

Contents

CONTENTS

Section 2: Writing Fiction

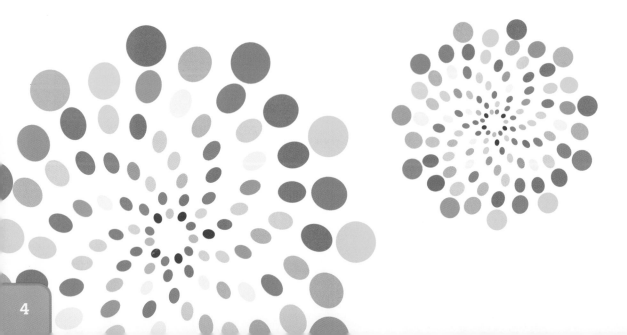

Section 3: Writing Non-Fiction

Section 4: Writing about Texts

Introduction

Welcome to an entirely new edition of *Writing to 14*, which has been rebuilt from the ground up!

I've taken the insights we have developed in recent years into how grammatical knowledge can build confidence in writing, tested it with the students I teach and written a textbook to put the ideas into action.

The result is a textbook that takes a much more explicit approach to developing students' understanding of grammar and style points, and helps them to apply them effectively and reflect on them critically. The aim, quite simply, is to help our students to become significantly better writers.

Structure

The structure of the book is entirely new. We begin with **Building Blocks of Writing** – the skills and approaches that successful writers routinely use to create their texts. Each unit introduces the essential skills, gives students modes to learn from and practice tasks to hone them, and then provides an extended assignment to extend and develop their writing with precision and accuracy.

Next we take students through the range of text-types and genres they are likely to encounter as writers, within English and other subjects, in **Writing Fiction** and **Writing Non-Fiction**. The grammatical knowledge from **Building Blocks of Writing** underpins the approach here, along with real-life samples which students encounter as models.

Finally, we have the **Writing about Texts** section. This section includes information on how to write about other texts, including poetry, non-fiction texts and comparing texts. The task of writing about texts, rather than writing texts, is something that students are frequently asked to do in lessons but without always having guidance and models. This section provides an essential step in consolidating understanding of what constitutes good writing.

Throughout the book, sample student responses are used to build students' understanding of the grammatical and stylistic conventions of different text types. We know from experience that students benefit not only from seeing actual examples of real-life texts, such as newspaper articles and extracts from novels, but they also gain a huge amount when asked to respond to, and critique, the writing of their peers. This can build their confidence in seeing what they themselves may be capable of.

Features

Throughout the units, key grammatical terms are highlighted and explained on the page, ensuring that the text is accessible for all students; the book also contains a detailed **Glossary** at the end, which explains all of the relevant grammatical terms. The idea throughout is that the skills and knowledge that successful writers implicitly use should be made explicit to our students.

There is also a **Hints for Success** feature, which offers advice for students approaching the extended writing tasks, and a **Word Booster** feature, which explicitly highlights the kind of vocabulary that students should use in their writing. **Word Booster** is about expanding vocabulary. It is designed to help those students who say 'I don't know what to write' by tuning them into the right register and appropriate vocabulary for whatever the writing task.

Writer's Toolkit

The book concludes with a completely new reference section, which is designed to support independent learning and self-correction. This includes information on tricky spellings and common errors, which provides a useful reference point for the kinds of questions students might have about daily English usage.

Conclusion

This is, as you can see, a new book for a new approach to developing writing. It has been written to reflect the latest research into writing and to prepare students for further English study.

As ever, a textbook will never replace the enthusiasm and commitment of a great teacher – but I hope that you will find it an indispensible resource in your classroom as you coach, chivvy and inspire your own students to become better writers. My very best wishes to you during the process.

Geoff Barton

Reviewing Your Strengths and Weaknesses

Big Picture

Human beings are unique. We use language to communicate a huge range of thoughts and ideas. Even if you don't feel very confident about the way you use language, you probably know more than 35,000 words! However, before you can become a more confident, accurate and powerful writer, you need to assess your own strengths and weaknesses in your language use.

Skills

- Develop a better understanding of your strengths and weaknesses as a writer.

Getting started

1 Take five minutes to reflect on your own language use, using the following prompts. You can discuss your answers with a partner, make notes or write short paragraphs in response to the questions.

   a According to your parents, when did you first speak? What were your first words? Which books and television programmes were you especially fond of when you were younger?

   b When you went to primary school, what do you recall about learning to read and write? Which subjects did you feel most and least confident in? Which teacher had the biggest influence upon you and why?

   c As you grew older, which parts of language did you become more and less confident in? For example, did you begin to worry about spelling? Were you confident about talking in front of the class? Did you like being asked to read aloud?

Building your skills

Each of us has our own special way of talking. There are certain words that we all use frequently and certain **fillers** that we use when we can't think of a word – for example: 'you know', 'OK?', 'right?' or 'like'. We can often tell who is speaking even when we can't see them – we recognize them from their **idiolect** (a person's speech habits). As we get older we change the way we speak, and people often move their voices up and down to convey meaning more effectively (this is called **intonation**).

> **Glossary**
>
> **filler:** words that are used in conversation to fill pauses, e.g. *er, um* and *y'know*
>
> **idiolect:** a person's personal speech habits and patterns, including the words they use and their accent
>
> **intonation:** the rise and fall of a person's voice when speaking

1 Create a grid that contains information about your own idiolect. Include:

a words (including fillers) you use often

b words you avoid because you aren't sure you fully understand them

c words you find difficult to spell

d a description of the way you speak (how you think your voice sounds to other people)

e language situations you like or hate – for example, spelling work, giving talks, group discussion, reading aloud, writing in class.

Developing your writing

Write an assignment about your language history.

Start by interviewing someone at home who knew you as a baby and toddler. Find out more about your early language use from this person. Ask them:

- what kind of noises you made before you said any words; for example, did you often laugh or cry – or shriek?
- what your early words were
- how talkative you were as a child
- how you learned to read and what books you enjoyed reading
- how and when you began to write.

Structure your response under these two headings:

- My early use of language
- Early literacy: how I began to read and write

Hints for Success

- Be as precise as you can about what age you were, what words you said and what books you read. Specific examples often make your writing more interesting.

- Find alternatives to starting every sentence with *I was*. Instead write *My early words included…* and *My mum describes my early language as being…*

Word Booster

Try to use some of the following words to make your response more specific and informative:

- includes ● seems ● possibly ● unclear ● memorable

Learning More About How Writing Works

Big Picture   This unit teaches you more about writing – something that human beings invented thousands of years ago. After looking at how writing developed, you can look in more detail at your own attitude to writing.

Skills   ● Explore some of the features of written language.

Getting started

The alphabet was invented more than 3000 years ago, but there are of course other forms which are used to communicate, such as Chinese pictograms and Morse Code.

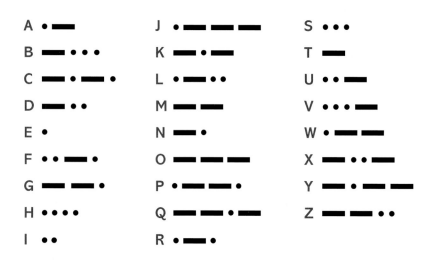

Take a look at the Morse Code diagram on the left. It was developed as a way of communicating over long distances – either by sound (short and long tapping sounds) or by using flashing lights.

1   Think of a sentence to describe a programme you watched on television over the past few days. Write it out in Morse Code.

2   Then, with a partner, see if you can decode each other's messages.

Building your skills

Codes are a good way of reminding ourselves how we first learned to write – by recognizing written symbols and learning their meanings.

The Egyptians started using hieroglyphics more than 7000 years ago. They did not use capital letters or have spaces between words and the signs could be read either from left to right or right to left.

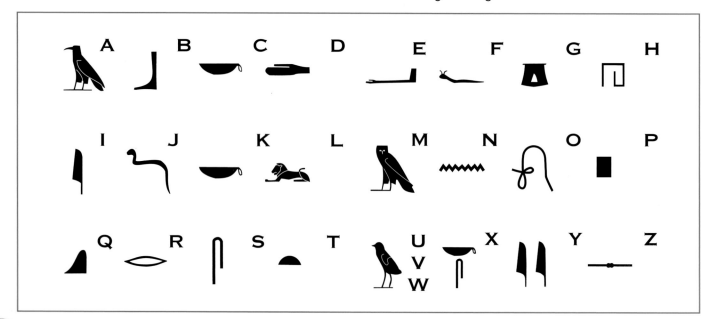

1 Working on your own or with a partner, work out what these statements, written using hieroglyphics, say:

a

b

2 Now write a sentence of your own using hieroglyphics. Swap your message with a partner and try to decode each other's sentence.

3 What were the main problems in reading the hieroglyphics? Was it easier to code or decode language? Did you feel you got better at it with practice? Write a short paragraph reflecting on the process.

The easiest way to create a code is to swap around the letters of the alphabet, replacing them with other letters. Certain letters occur more frequently than others and so you can soon start to make guesses at which letters have been replaced with which.

A = Q	B =	C =	D =	E =	F =	G =
H =	I =	J =	K =	L =	M =	N =
O =	P =	Q =	R =	S =	T =	U =
V =	W =	X =	Y =	Z =		

Choose a paragraph of text, either from this book or your own writing, and write it in your new code. Then give it to a partner to see whether they can work out the meaning. Use a grid like the one above to crack your partner's code.

Hints for Success

Make some informed guesses about your partner's coded text using these tips. Look especially for:

- common one-letter words like *a* and *I*
- common two-letter words like *is*, *of* and *an*
- common three-letter words like *the* and *and*.

Using Punctuation to Make Your Writing Clearer

Big Picture People sometimes get confused about why we use **punctuation**. This unit shows you why our most basic punctuation marks developed and how they help us to write more clearly.

Skills
- Understand the purpose of punctuation.

Getting started

Punctuation developed when human beings started to write things down. One of the most basic forms of punctuation is one we take for granted – spaces between words.

In other languages – for example, Chinese and Japanese – spaces aren't used.

1 Read this text which has no punctuation:

> weservehotandcoldfoodandawidevarietyofsnacksalldayinour
> brightlydecoratedandwelcomingrestaurantwithinthefamilyareaisa
> largecarpetedspacewhichissetasideforplayingwitharangeoftoys
> thataresuitableforbothgirlsandboysallofourfoodishomecookedand
> useslocalproduce

a If you were separating these words to create sentences, how many sentences do you think there should be?

b How many full stops and capital letters would you add?

c Compare your responses with a partner.

d Discuss which words were the most difficult to identify and why you think this was.

Glossary

comma: (,) a punctuation mark used to show a pause in a sentence and to separate items in a list, e.g. *I like computers, football, tennis and playing my guitar.*

exclamation mark: (!) a punctuation mark, used at the end of a sentence, to show shock

full stop: (.) a punctuation mark used to mark the end of a sentence

punctuation: signs used in written language to separate elements in sentences and to signal an attitude or relationship

question mark: (?) a punctuation mark, used at the end of a sentence, to show that a question is being asked

Building your skills

1 Imagine an alien from outer space is learning to read English for the first time. Your job is to teach the alien about basic punctuation marks. Read through the list below and, for each one, write down a description which explains when we would use that form of punctuation.

PUNCTUATION MARK	EXPLANATION
Spaces	We use spaces to…
Capital letters	
Full stops	
Commas	
Question marks	
Exclamation marks	

Developing your writing

Read the text below. It has been written without any punctuation marks. Using your knowledge, rewrite the text with accurate punctuation.

the room looked terrifying what was in there i decided that i had to explore it even though i had been warned to stay away i moved closer then i heard a sound i paused listened and waited then I heard a crash an almighty sound from inside the room told me that my worst nightmare was happening there was no doubt after all these years the place was beginning to fall apart i grabbed my backpack helmet and bike and sped off

Hints for Success

Make sure you understand the difference between commas and full stops. You should use commas as pauses within sentences or to separate items in a list; full stops should come at the end of a sentence. Check you have done this correctly.

Using Colons to Improve Your Writing

Big Picture Basic punctuation marks help you to express your ideas clearly and accurately. Advanced punctuation – **colons** and semi-colons – can help you to express a wider range of ideas. This unit shows you how to use colons.

Skills
- Understand what colons are and become more confident in using them.

Getting started

Colons look like this :

A good way of understanding colons is to think of them as headlights on a car. They point ahead, helping the reader to know what's coming up. They are useful at the start of lists and leading into quotations. They are also useful in sentences to build a feeling of **suspense** or **tension**.

Glossary

colon: (:) a punctuation mark used before lists and quotations

suspense or **tension:** the way writers hold back information to keep readers guessing what will happen next

Here are some examples:

> **Colons before lists:**
>
> When I go shopping today, I'll be buying a range of presents: socks for Grandpa, some chocolates for Mum and a treat for my hamster.

> **Colons before quotations:**
>
> At the start of the play the audience learns that Macbeth is a hero from the way he is introduced by the Sergeant: 'brave Macbeth – well he deserves that name'.

> **Colons to build suspense:**
>
> As she walked home towards her house, she sensed that something terrible was about to happen: she was right.

Building your skills

Practice is the only way to see whether you can use colons correctly. Try the following activities to test your colon use:

1 Write a sentence using a colon before a list. Make the subject about your journey home and what you see.

2 Write a sentence about a novel or poem you have recently read in class and use a colon to introduce a quotation.

3 Use a colon to build suspense. Write a sentence describing someone walking around a corner, sensing that something or someone is waiting for them.

Developing your writing

Review your writing. Which of the three colon tasks was the easiest and which was the most difficult? Choose the area you feel weakest in – using colons before lists, before quotations or to build suspense – and practise the skill further as homework.

Hints for Success

● Learning a new skill takes time and effort. Practise and get feedback from your teacher and classmates.

● Read the work of other writers – in books and newspapers – and notice how they use colons.

Using Semi-Colons in Your Writing

Big Picture **Semi-colons** are another advanced form of punctuation. They can help make your ideas clearer for your reader, but they need to be handled with care. They aren't the same as commas or full stops or colons. They have their own special function.

Skills ● Understand how and when to use semi-colons in your writing.

Getting started A semi-colon (;) looks like a comma with a full stop above it – and that is a bit of a clue as to what they do in a sentence.

What do you know about semi-colons? Have you ever seen them used? If so, in what kind of texts – instructions, novels, poems, posters, reports? Do they appear in formal or informal texts? Do you see them used within speech marks to punctuate what people are saying?

1 Write down, in a sentence, what you already understand about why and how semi-colons are used.

2 Here are some examples of sentences that contain semi-colons. On your own or with a partner, try to work out how these semi-colons are working differently from a full stop or comma.

> **1** I like music; I play the guitar, piano and drums.

> **2** I have been taught by several brilliant teachers such as: Geography teacher, Mrs Fawcett; History teacher, Mr Small; and English teacher, Miss Mahmood.

> **3** During the day I love hot sunny weather; at night I love the sound of rain.

Building your skills

A semi-colon is a pause somewhere between a full stop and a comma. This is easy to remember because it is made up of both punctuation marks – a comma below and a full stop above.

There are two main uses of the semi-colon. The first is to join sentences and **phrases** that feel separate but have a related theme. Instead of a semi-colon you could often put the **conjunction** 'and' between the sentences or phrases. Look again at the first example to see this at work.

The second use is to separate items in a list which are longer than a word or two. The list usually starts with a colon and the semi-colons then separate the phrases. Look at the second example to see this.

1   Look again at the third example and explain, in your own words, why the writer has used a semi-colon rather than a comma or full stop.

Glossary

conjunction: a word that links phrases or clauses together, aslo known as **connectives**

phrase: a group of two or more words that does not include a main verb

semi-colon: (;) a punctuation mark which can be used instead of a full stop to separate two sentences that are closely related to each other, or to separate items in a list

Developing your writing

1   Here's the opening of a paragraph about school life. Add three semi-colons to the extract, where you think they are needed.

Some people love school, some people hate it. Personally, I have always liked the following parts of school life: meeting and mixing with people from different backgrounds, learning a range of skills that I probably couldn't learn at home, getting to be taught by people who are often experts in their subject.

2   Write your own paragraph of four sentences to show that you can use semi-colons to link separate but connected items and to separate longer items in a list.

Hints for Success

- This is tough, technical stuff; don't give up if you find it difficult.

- Look back at the examples so that you are clear on how semi-colons work differently from commas and full stops.

Using Standard English

Big Picture   We change the way we speak and write in different situations. This unit looks at **Standard English**, the form of English that is used most in school, on television and radio, and in other formal situations, such as in a courtroom.

Skills
- Learn more about how and when to use Standard English.

Getting started

1   Read the text below. Mark is talking about Charlie Chaplin, the star of silent movies in the early 20th century:

> I always remember a story about Charlie Chaplin. They reckon even when he was rich, he used to hide food and store food. I can understand that. Because you always think you're ganning to be left with naught again, aren't you? It's in the back of your mind. But I, we, we bought our house and, uh, it's the best thing we done, like. And I'm, you've got to be content with what you've got, haven't you? You know.

   a   How can you tell that this is spoken rather than written English?
   b   Where do you think Mark might come from?

2   Now look more closely at the words Mark uses. He uses words from his own regional **dialect** – these are words that would be understood by people in that area.

   Copy the grid below; complete the grid by thinking of a word that has the same meaning as each dialect word, but would be understood by English speakers in most parts of the world.

DIALECT WORDS	STANDARD ENGLISH WORDS
reckon	
ganning	
naught	
we done	

Glossary

dialect: a variety of language used in a particular location or by a particular group, e.g. American English

Standard English: the form of English that is considered the 'norm' and is typically used in formal situations

Building your skills

Most areas have dialect words for certain topics. These are sometimes used by people who are older or younger than us; for example, your grandparents might use different words than you do.

1   Look at the topics below and write down any dialect words that other people in your family or friends might use. Think of words that belong to your area but would not be known by all English speakers. See how many 'local' words you can think of from your regional dialect for:

- saying something is really good
- saying something is bad
- bread rolls
- passageways between houses
- family members (for example, meaning father or grandmother)
- attractive

2   Use a spider diagram to group all the words together. In the middle of the diagram write down where you live.

Developing your writing

Write three paragraphs about the way you use language in the different situations outlined below. Think about the words you use for each of these situations.

- What kind of spoken language do you use at home with your family?
- What kind of spoken language do you use at school? Is the language that you use when talking to your friends different to the language you use when talking to teachers? How?
- What kind of written language do you use at home and school? How does it differ?

Hints for Success

- The secret for this writing task is to be as precise as you can. Try to mention specific words you use in different situations.

- Show that you can reflect on your language use by commenting on how you change the way you speak or write in different situations, and why.

- Try to write your paragraphs in a way that will interest the reader. You might start like this: *I definitely use spoken language differently at home from when I am at school. At home, I…*

Creating Textual Rhythm in Your Writing

Big Picture Good writers create rhythm in their writing. They do this by using words and **sentences** that are interesting for us to read, which sound good inside our head or when we read them aloud.

Skills
- Develop the style of your own writing to give it a more interesting rhythm.

Getting started

Here are two text extracts written by Sam, a Year 9 student. He was asked to describe a place he remembered from childhood. As an experiment, he wrote about the same place in two different styles.

Compare the two texts and answer the questions below.

Glossary

sentence: a unit of meaning that makes sense on its own; it begins with a capital letter and ends with a full stop, question mark or exclamation mark, e.g. *The girl caught the ball.*

Text A

I remember 'the den'. It was in the woods. It was not far from my house. I would go there with friends. We would watch people walk past but they wouldn't notice us. We used to hang out there. My mum didn't know about it. It was a place we could hide. It doesn't exist now.

Text B

I remember 'the den' in some woods near my house. With friends, I would go there and then sit and watch people walking past without them noticing us. It was a place just to hang out. My mum would be shocked to know about it, but it was just a hiding-place. It's gone now.

1 What is your first impression: which text, A or B, is more interesting?

2 Write down three main differences you notice between the two texts.

3 If you were Sam's teacher, what advice would you give him to improve each version of his text?

Building your skills

1 Look at the words Sam uses in text A. Which is the most unusual or interesting word?

2 Now do the same for text B – which is the most unusual or interesting word in this paragraph?

3 **a** Look at the length of the sentences in text A. Work out the average length of Sam's sentences by counting all the words in the whole text and then dividing that number by the number of sentences.
   b Do the same for text B.

4 Most people find text B more interesting to read than text A. Based on studying the texts, say why you think this might be.

Developing your writing

Write 250 words about your journey to school each day. Try to make your sentences as varied as possible, and use interesting words, in order to create textual rhythm.

Hints for Success

- Vary the length of your sentences to create textual rhythm. Use short sentences for dramatic impact and longer sentences to provide more detail.

- Use paragraphs in your writing.

- Use a range of exciting words which help the reader to picture the journey in their mind.

Making Your Sentences More Varied

Big Picture This unit continues to build your skills in writing more interesting sentences, in order to keep your readers engaged. A good way to add interest to your writing is by varying the length of your sentences: writing some sentences that are long and some that are short.

Skills
- Learn how to write sentences of different lengths and complexity.

Getting started

When a text uses sentences of roughly the same length it can become quite boring, even when the subject should be interesting. For example, read the following text, written by Alia in Year 9:

> ### Being followed?
> I was walking home. I heard a sound behind me. I paused and listened. There was no sound any more. I decided to carry on home. There was that sound again. I stopped walking again. Again there was no sound.

Most of us like mysteries, so the subject matter of this should make us want to read on. Why doesn't this story hook our attention?

1 If you were Alia's teacher, what advice would you give her? Look at the statements below and put them in order, starting with those you most agree with.

> *A You need to describe the scene in more detail.*
>
> *B You need to use some longer words.*
>
> *C You need to vary the length of your sentences — some shorter, some longer.*
>
> *D You need to join your sentences up with words like 'and' and 'but'.*
>
> *E You need to stop using 'I' at the start of so many sentences.*

Building your skills

There are two main ways to add ideas to sentences.

Technique 1: Compound sentences

One way is to write **compound sentences** where you link ideas with conjunctions such as 'and', 'but' or 'or'; for example:

> I like going shopping *but* I don't really have lots of money *and* that can be quite frustrating *but* I still go with my friends.

Technique 2: Subordinate clauses

Compound sentences can become very long because you can keep adding another conjunction and idea to the end of the sentence.

The other way of adding ideas to sentences is by adding **subordinate clauses** to make a **complex sentence**. There are different ways of doing this, but one way is to use subordinating conjunctions. These are linking words that allow you to add background information to a sentence; for example:

I go shopping *because* I like spending time with friends.

As I like being with friends, I often go shopping.

Although I haven't got much money, I still go shopping with friends.

When I go shopping, it's being with friends that is most fun.

Glossary

complex sentence: a sentence containing a subordinate clause

subordinate clause: a clause that does not make sense on its own, e.g. *When I run*

1 Look at the conjunctions in the grid below. Also included is the purpose of each conjunction – what function they perform in a sentence. Try rewriting Alia's paragraph about being followed using longer sentences and some of these subordinating conjunctions.

SUBORDINATING CONJUNCTIONS	PURPOSE
As, while, before, until	To express time
Because, so	To explain cause and effect
Unless, except, as long as, yet	To qualify
Although, unlike, whereas	To contrast

Developing your writing

Think about the worst journey of your life. It might be a time when you were in a bad traffic jam, a time you felt ill or a journey to a holiday destination that went horribly wrong. Write 250 words describing the journey in a way that will interest your reader.

Hints for Success

- Use some short, simple sentences for dramatic effect (e.g. *It was the worst journey of my life*).

- Use some of the subordinating conjunctions listed above to link your ideas.

- Choose words that will appeal to the reader's senses and will help them to see, hear and smell the scenes you describe.

Using Relative Clauses to Add Detail

Big Picture
So far in this book we have seen that good writing is often a result of using a range of interesting words in varied sentences. This unit shows you another way to make your sentences more engaging, by using **relative clauses**.

Skills
- Learn to use relative clauses to add detail to your sentences.

Getting started
Read the following piece of writing by Stephen in Year 8. He was asked to write about a pet. What do you think of it?

Glossary

relative clause: groups of words that begin with a relative pronoun (*that, which, who, whose*), e.g. *The cake, which was delivered, arrived in time for the party.*

> The cat was nasty looking. It was sitting by the fire. It was glaring at me through its evil eyes. The fire was crackling loudly. We were at my grandma's house. It smelt of stale cooking. The cat just sat there and glared. I didn't move, in case it attacked. The cat seemed to be thinking that I was an enemy. It seemed to be thinking it should protect grandma. It looked like it was going to attack me at any moment.

1 What do you like about Stephen's writing?

2 If you were Stephen's teacher, what would you tell him to do in order to improve his paragraph?

Building your skills
Relative clauses are groups of words that begin with a relative pronoun, such as:

- that
- which
- who
- whose.

Relative pronouns help you to add background information about a person, thing or place without starting a new sentence, like this:

TWO SEPARATE SENTENCES	ONE SENTENCE USING A RELATIVE PRONOUN
The cat sat by the fire. Its eyes looked evil.	The cat, *whose* eyes looked evil, sat by the fire.
The fire crackled noisily. It threw out a tremendous heat.	The fire, *which* threw out a tremendous heat, crackled noisily.

1   Practise creating sentences using relative pronouns. Copy the grid below. Change each set of two sentences in the left-hand column into one sentence using a relative pronoun.

TWO SEPARATE SENTENCES	ONE SENTENCE USING A RELATIVE PRONOUN (THAT, WHICH, WHO, WHOSE)
My house is a dump. I have lived in it for seven years.	
The boy's older brother was bad tempered. He had stinking breath.	
Frank was looking worried as he peered at the clock. His car would simply not start.	
The room looked cold and empty. It had terrified me since I was a child.	
My computer crashed again. It seems to have a life of its own.	

Developing your writing

Write a paragraph or two, of 150 words in total, describing your earliest memories of school. Use relative pronouns in three of your sentences to add background detail.

Hints for Success

- Your sentences will become more interesting if you write some which include relative pronouns – but don't overdo it! Use some short, simple sentences too.

- Remember that good writing comes from choosing words that help the reader to see or hear or smell what you are describing.

Expanding Noun Phrases to Add Detail

Big Picture
One way of making your writing more interesting and precise is by adding detail to **noun phrases**. This sounds more technical than it is in practice, as you will discover in this unit.

Skills
- Learn to expand noun phrases correctly in order to add detail to your writing.

Getting started

One key ingredient in good writing is that it should include detail about the things that we describe.

Glossary

determiner: a word that comes before a noun to show how the noun is being used, e.g. *the, a, some*.

noun: a thing, name or place, e.g. *panda, teacher, book, Ravi, London*

noun phrase: a noun made up of more than one word, e.g. *the elephant*

post-modify: add description after a noun

pre-modify: add description before a noun

1 Imagine you have been asked to describe an abandoned house in the middle of some woods. Create a spider diagram that includes 15 words that you might use to describe the scene. Think of words that will help to illustrate the sights, sounds, smells and textures of the abandoned house.

Building your skills

Noun phrases are the groups of words we use to name things, for example 'the man' or 'her desk'. The examples below show how you can expand a basic noun phrase, such as 'the fish', to add more detail. You can **pre-modify** a noun phrase (put words in front of it) and **post-modify** it (put words after it).

- the fish
- *my* fish
- *my new* fish
- *my new* fish *called Trevor*
- *my new* fish *called Trevor who's in his bowl*

You can pre-modify a noun phrase by:

● changing the **determiner** in front of the noun to make it more personal, e.g. changing 'the' or 'a' to 'my' or 'her'
● changing the determiner to make it plural, e.g. 'some' or 'many'
● adding adjectives between the determiner ('the') and the noun ('bike'), e.g. 'the *speedy* bike'.

You can post-modify a noun phrase by:

● adding a phrase that begins with 'in', 'of', 'under' or 'on' after the noun phrase, e.g. 'the desk *in Lei's room*'
● adding a phrase that begins with a relative pronoun ('who', 'that', 'which', 'whose') after the noun, e.g. 'the boy *who ate too much*'.

1 Think of two ways of pre-modifying the noun phrase 'the abandoned house' and two ways of post-modifying it, using the grid below.

PRE-MODIFY	NOUN PHRASE	POST-MODIFY
Add: • a determiner instead of 'the' (e.g. 'my', 'his', 'an') • another adjective to describe the house.	(the) abandoned house	Add: • a phrase starting with 'in', 'on', 'under', 'near' or 'within' • a phrase starting with a relative pronoun such as 'which', 'that', 'who'.

2 Look at the noun phrases below. Choose three of these noun phrases and add detail by pre- and post-modifying them:

● the computer   ● the ravens
● a sweetshop   ● a football match
● the end   ● the friends

Developing your writing

Look at the room you are in now and write a paragraph of detailed description using some expanded noun phrases. Underline each example of where you have pre-modified or post-modified a **noun**.

Hints for Success

● Remember to think of details and senses: consider the colours, textures, sounds and smells of the room.

● You could start your paragraph with: *This familiar room in... seems...*

Using Front-Shifting in Your Writing

Big Picture

One of the key ingredients of successful writing is that it is interesting. Readers *want* to read it: it holds their attention. One way to make your writing more engaging is by using a technique called **front-shifting**. This enables us to move the main information in a **clause** or sentence further forward, making our writing easier to follow and clearer.

Skills

- Manipulate sentences so that key details are front-shifted, making them clearer or more interesting.

Getting started

1 Look at the grid below. In each row, there are two similar sentences. Compare each version and then look at the questions that follow.

VERSION A	VERSION B
I started feeling ill on the second day of the holiday.	On the second day of the holiday, I started feeling ill.
I really enjoyed the film now I think about it.	Now I think about it, I really enjoyed the film.
He started feeling sick as soon as the journey began.	As soon as the journey began, he started feeling sick.
The bonfire will be better the bigger we make it.	The bigger we make it, the better the bonfire will be.

    a In your own words, explain what the writer does differently in the two versions of the sentences.

    b Choose one example and say which version you think is easier to understand. Explain why.

> **Glossary**
>
> **clause:** a group of words which includes a subject and a verb, e.g. *When I run in the evening*
>
> **front-shifting:** moving an element of a sentence to the front, in order to emphasize it, e.g. *That car we saw – there was something suspicious about it.*

Building your skills

Front-shifting sounds more complicated than it is. It is the way we move an idea to the front of a clause or sentence. This can give the idea more emphasis, make it clearer or help to create a contrast with what comes later.

1 Look at the sentences below and, for each one, practise front-shifting the highlighted section. Write out each sentence using the new order.

    a There will be trouble at the end of the lesson if you don't pay attention now.

    b I will be happy when the job is done.

c There are two players waiting at the far end of the penalty box.

d I grew up in Manchester and in Manchester I will die.

e He forgot to explain what he meant in the middle of his talk.

Developing your writing

Describe the view from your bedroom window.

It would be easy for every sentence to begin with a similar pattern like this:

- The view from my bedroom window is…
- I can see…
- There are lots of…

Instead, use front-shifting to change the sentence patterns:

- In the garden…, I…
- Under the fence…, there…
- If you look…, you…
- Further back, you…

Hints for Success

- If it helps, underline the words you have used as the front-shifted element.

- Front-shifting is just one technique that writers use. Although you are practising it here, you shouldn't use it in every sentence you write.

Using Synonyms to Make Your Writing Interesting

Big Picture You might think that becoming better at writing always means using longer sentences and bigger words. In fact, the best writers frequently use short sentences and the words they choose aren't long and complicated, they are just more precise. Often writers use **synonyms** – words with a similar meaning – to add variety to their work.

Skills ● Improve your use of vocabulary by choosing synonyms (words of similar meaning).

Getting started

You know more words than you realize. Language experts estimate that by the time we are adults we have around 60,000 words in our **vocabulary**. Some of these words are in our passive vocabulary: we recognize them when we see or hear the words used; others are in our active vocabulary: we use them frequently in our speech and writing.

> **Glossary**
>
> **synonym:** a word with a similar meaning to another word, e.g. *large* and *bulky* are synonyms of *big*
>
> **vocabulary:** the range of words known by a person

Here is a group of words which all mean 'nice'.

admirable	amiable	attractive	charming
cordial	delightful	genial	inviting
lovely	obliging	OK	pleasant

1 a Using a grid like the one below, categorize how well you know each of the words above.

DON'T KNOW THE WORD AT ALL	I RECOGNIZE THE WORD	IT'S A WORD I KNOW WELL AND USE

b Use a dictionary to find definitions of the words that you don't know.

2 Look at the sentences below. Finish each sentence off by using an appropriate word from the list.

a The view from the hillside was…

b The behaviour of my auntie was…

c Being with my friends was…

Building your skills

One important skill when writing is to choose the right word for the right context. Sometimes you will want a formal word and sometimes a more informal one, depending on who you are talking or writing to.

Look at the list of words below meaning 'big'.

ample	colossal	enormous	extensive	gigantic
great	hefty	huge	hulking	immense
large	massive	roomy	tremendous	vast

1 Choose five of the words and put them in order of most informal to most formal.

2 Choose three different words from the list above. Write three sentences to demonstrate that you understand the meaning of each one.

Hints for Success

When you think about formal and informal language, think of your audience. With friends you know well, you are likely to be more informal. With adults you don't know well, you are likely to be more formal.

Developing your writing

Write a paragraph describing yourself lost in a forest at night. Imagine you sense a creature that you cannot recognize moving about among the trees.

Make your writing atmospheric (formal word) and creepy (informal word), using at least five of the synonyms for 'nasty' that are given below.

awful	disagreeable
foul	ghastly
gruesome	horrible
loathsome	noxious
repellent	repugnant
revolting	sickening
stinking	unpleasant
vile	

Using Non-Finite Clauses in Your Writing

Big Picture **Non-finite clauses** are used by confident writers to express their ideas more effectively. This unit shows you how to use them.

Skills
- Use non-finite clauses to make your writing more varied.

Getting started

Clauses are the building blocks of sentences. They are groups of words which have a **subject** and a **verb**. When clauses are finite we can answer questions about who, when, and how many – like this:

Finite clause: She arrived at home.

QUESTION	ANSWER
Who?	She
When?	In the past
How many?	One person (she)

1 To show that you understand finite clauses, answer the same questions ('Who?', 'When?' and 'How many?') for these three examples:

   a I stayed at home.

   b They will travel later.

   c He hates his food.

2 Non-finite clauses are different. They allow you to put some additional information in a sentence. Try answering the questions 'Who?', 'When?' and 'How many?' for the clauses below and you'll see it's not possible.

Hoping the day would improve,…   Throwing another snowball,…

Building your skills

Non-finite clauses help you to avoid repeating yourself. Instead of saying 'Dan was hoping the day would improve and he watched the horizon', you can say 'Hoping the day would improve, Dan watched the horizon'.

> **Glossary**
>
> **finite clause:** a clause that contains a main verb and can stand on its own as a sentence
>
> **non-finite clause:** a clause that does not contain a main verb and cannot stand on its own as a sentence
>
> **subject:** the thing or person in a sentence which carries out the action, e.g. *fish* is the subject in the following sentence: *The fish swam around the tank*.
>
> **verb:** a word that tells you about the action in a sentence, e.g. *swam* is the verb in the following sentence: *The fish swam around the tank*.

1 Look at these non-finite clauses which begin with *-ing* verbs. Make up a second half for each sentence.

    a Waking in the middle of the night,…

    b Worrying about the day ahead,…

    c Putting his old clothes to one side,…

    d Rushing across the playground,…

Hints for Success

- So that your sentence makes sense, the second clause must start with the subject of the sentence (the person who carries out the action); for example: *Running for the bus, <u>the girl</u> dropped her headphones.*

Developing your writing

Imagine that you are trapped in an old abandoned school. Write a paragraph or two describing what happens to you and how you are feeling. In a passage of writing, you won't want all of your sentences to follow the same structure, so practise writing using a mixture of different types of sentence.

Use:

- some short simple sentences (e.g. 'Where was I?')
- some longer sentences in which you join clauses with 'and' or 'but' (e.g. 'I looked around and noticed something there')
- some non-finite clauses that begin with an *-ing* verb ('Listening carefully, I noticed…').

Using Adjectives and Adverbs

A large number of writers use too many **adjectives** and **adverbs** in their writing, thinking it makes their work more interesting. In fact, these can just 'clog up' a description. This unit is about when to use adjectives and adverbs and when not to!

Skills
- Know when to use adjectives and adverbs.

Getting started

Adjectives modify nouns. That means they give more detail to objects, people and places. They might describe:

- size ('massive')
- colour ('blue')
- quality ('superb')
- quantity ('numerous')
- type ('English').

Glossary

adjective: a describing word used to give more information about a noun, e.g. *The beautiful diamond sparkled magnificently.*

adverb: a word which gives more information about how an action is carried out, e.g. *The beautiful diamond sparkled magnificently.* Adverbs often end in -ly

Adverbs modify verbs; they give more detail to activities and processes. They often (but not always) end with -ly. They might describe:

- manner ('happily')
- time ('afterwards')
- frequency ('most')
- place ('here')
- attitude ('curiously').

Look at the two sentences below. The first contains no adjectives or adverbs; the second has many.

> This is the car for you.

> This is the *best, most expensive, exciting* and *arguably highest-performing saloon* car for you.

1 Practise modifying these sentences by adding adjectives and adverbs.

   a The _____ house that sits _____ at the edge of the _____ forest.

   b The _____ owl looked up _____ from the _____ tree-stump where she was _____ sitting.

   c _____ children ran _____ out of the _____ school building and into the _____ yard.

Building your skills

Effective writers know when to use adjectives and adverbs. Sometimes it is better to have a simple sentence built around a well-chosen verb. For example:

'The man *yelled* in terror.' (powerful verb)   is more powerful than

'The small timid man called out loudly in massive terror.'
(weak verb with lots of modifying adjectives and adverbs)

The secret is to choose modifying words which surprise the reader or sit unexpectedly with the verb or noun.

The dark house loomed over me.	is more vivid than	The big house was in front of me.
The heroic child wept in silent relief.	is more vivid than	The brave child started to cry because she was relieved.
The scrawny cat looked up at me hopefully.	is more vivid than	The hungry cat looked up at me wanting some food.

1 Practise using adjectives and adverbs by describing your bedroom. Note the sounds, colours and textures and then write your description. Aim to write some simple sentences, as well as some which include more detail.

Developing your writing

Write an extended piece of descriptive writing: imagine you are walking home from visiting a friend; it is night time and you start to sense that you are being followed. Use vivid, well-chosen adjectives and adverbs to add detail, as well as a mixture of simple and complex sentences.

Hints for Success

- Remember that the skill is to know when to use adjectives and adverbs and when not to!

- Try to use interesting and unexpected adjectives and adverbs, rather than the first words that come into your mind.

Creating Cohesion in a Text

Big Picture   When we write, we usually want our readers to be able to understand our text easily. Writers aim to be clear. One way of doing this is to make sure that there is **cohesion** across sentences and paragraphs – that the links between our ideas are clear.

Skills   ● Use different techniques to achieve cohesion.

Getting started

One way of understanding cohesion is to read a text which does it badly. Read this student's description of his visit to the city of Shanghai, China.

> I was impressed by the amazing train system that goes from the airport to the city in Shanghai. It is an amazing place when you land and very large with loads of skyscrapers and when you get on it it travels at speeds of up to 300 kilometres per hour. It took us from the airport to the city in just 15 minutes and it was a stunning place to look around.

1 Look closely at the writing.

   a Which parts of it were difficult to follow?

   b Suggest two pieces of advice that would help make the paragraph clearer.

Building your skills

There are two ways that we can create cohesion in texts: using **personal pronouns** and **adverbials**.

Technique 1: Personal pronouns   Use personal pronouns clearly. Personal pronouns help us to avoid repeating ourselves. Without **pronouns**, a text would read like this:

> The cat is lying in front of the fire. The cat is comfortable.

Instead we write:

> The cat is lying in front of the fire. She is comfortable.

Glossary

adverbial: a group of words which act like an adverb in a sentence, describing how or when something happened, e.g. *Before the play…*

cohesion: the way ideas are linked within a text

pronoun: a word that takes the place of a noun in a sentence, e.g. *it, that, he*

personal pronoun: a pronoun that refers to a person, e.g. *I, you, me, they, us, we, her, him*

Pronouns include: 'he', 'she', 'it', 'they', 'them' and 'myself'. In writing, it's a problem if the reader cannot tell what the pronoun is referring to. For instance, it is unclear whether 'it' refers to the rabbit or the cage in the following example: 'The rabbit is sitting in its cage. *It* is huge.'

1 In the text below, it's difficult to understand who some of the personal pronouns are referring to. Rewrite this paragraph to make the writer's meaning clearer. You will need to take out some of the pronouns and replace them with nouns.

Radhika arrived at Lei's house and she said hello to her. 'Ready to go?' she said. 'Yes,' she replied and they set off – except Radhika remembered that she had left her keys at home. She remembered also that the twins said they wanted to come along. She ran back, picked them up, and set off again.

Technique 2: Adverbials

Use adverbials to link ideas within and across paragraphs. Adverbials are words and phrases that tell us more about how or when something happens. They can be single words – 'first', 'next', 'finally' – or phrases – 'in conclusion', 'as a result'.

2 Add adverbials to the instructions below, so that the reader can understand how and when to carry out the actions.

_____ take the tea-bag. _____ put the kettle on to boil. _____ prepare mugs or cups, plus milk and sugar. _____ the water is boiling hot, add it to the mug containing a tea-bag. _____ leave it to brew. _____ after a couple of minutes, remove the tea-bag.

Developing your writing

Practise using personal pronouns and adverbials to add clarity to your text. Choose one of the topics below and write a 150-word clear and cohesive paragraph on it:

● Advice on how to look after a certain kind of pet
● Advice on how to protect your personal information when on the Internet

Hints for Success

● Remember that your main aim is clarity.

● Use personal pronouns (*they*, *we*, *I*) and adverbials (*firstly*, *in conclusion*) to organize your ideas.

Using the Passive Voice in Formal Writing

Big Picture
When we first learn to write, we are usually encouraged to write in a personal style – writing about ourselves and our own experiences. One sign of developing as a writer is being able to write in a more impersonal style. This involves using 'I' and 'me' less; it can also mean using the **passive voice**.

Skills
- Understand how to use the passive voice.

Getting started

The passive voice is a writing technique that 'hides' the **agent** in a sentence (the person or thing who 'does' the action). The easiest way to see what this means is to compare two examples – one using the **active voice** and one using the passive.

ACTIVE VOICE	PASSIVE VOICE
I ripped the poster.	The poster got ripped.

1 In your own words, try to explain how the examples differ.

> **Glossary**
>
> **active voice:** a writing technique where the subject of the sentence performs the action; e.g. *He announced the news* (active) rather than *The news was announced by him* (passive)
>
> **agent:** the person or thing that performs the action described by a verb, e.g. *the snow* is the agent in the following sentences: *The snow fell heavily that night* and *Her path was covered by the snow*; the agent is also known as the **subject**
>
> **passive voice:** a writing technique that avoids emphasizing the agent/subject of the action, e.g. *The window was broken by the boy* (passive) rather than *The boy broke the window* (active)

Building your skills

The passive voice is often used in scientific writing and news reports. Here's an example of a scientific report written by a Year 9 student which uses the active voice and a revised version using the passive voice.

> **Text A: Active**
>
> We took the magnesium and we placed it in a test tube. Then we took the Bunsen burner and started to heat the magnesium.

> **Text B: Passive**
>
> The magnesium was placed in a test tube. Next it was heated using a Bunsen burner.

1   **a**   What do you like about text A?

   b   What do you like about text B?

   c   Why do you think that many scientists are encouraged to write in the passive style of text B: what are its advantages?

2   The passive 'hides' who the agent or subject of a sentence is. Copy the grid below and suggest who the agent might be for each example. The first one has been done for you.

SENTENCE IN PASSIVE VOICE	WHO IS THE AGENT?
Order was restored on the streets of the city.	The army or police
It was announced today that petrol prices will rise again.	
The factory was built in the 1920s.	
The film was declared a triumph.	

Developing your writing

Undertake a survey in your classroom so that you have some data for a report. Topics might include:

● A survey of people's favourite/least favourite song of the year
● A survey of people's favourite apps for smartphones

Then, to practise using the passive voice, write a 150-word report which includes these headings:

● The focus of the survey
● How the survey was carried out
● The results

Aim to avoid using the active voice ('I asked...', 'We discovered...') and instead use the passive ('Questions were asked...', 'Results showed...').

Hints for Success

● Refer back to the examples in the text to remind you what the passive voice looks like.

● Use subheadings to organize your report.

Word Booster

Try to use some of the following words to make your report more formal:

● Scientific and analytical verbs: *consider, investigate, analyse, suggest, present, undertake, prove, explore*

Using Hyponymy to Make Your Writing More Interesting

Big Picture This unit is all about words. You already know thousands of words, but accomplished writers often surprise us by choosing words very precisely. Although they may not know the technical terms, they are using **hyponyms** and **hypernyms** to make their writing richer and more interesting.

Skills
- Understand how hyponyms and hypernyms work.

Getting started Start by exploring the way we use vocabulary. Here are two pieces of writing describing traffic. Which is more interesting?

Text A

The city of Paris has some of the worst traffic jams in Europe. The roads can be jammed at certain times of the day as traffic tries to move around the city or through it. The worst of these traffic jams is on Tuesday mornings between eight and nine o'clock. Some research has shown that being in heavy traffic makes people living in Paris lose up to 70 hours a year.

Text B

Paris has some of the worst traffic jams in Europe. The roads can be gridlocked at key times of the day as vehicles attempt to move around or through the city. The peak times for congestion are Tuesday mornings between eight and nine o'clock. Some research suggests that this heavy traffic loses Parisians up to 70 hours a year in time.

1 Use a grid like this one to compare the way each writer uses vocabulary in the texts. Record how many times the following words occur in each text:

WORD	FREQUENCY OF USE IN TEXT A	FREQUENCY OF USE IN TEXT B
city		
traffic		
jams/jammed		
Paris		
worst		

2 What words does the writer of text B use to avoid repeating or writing:

    a 'traffic jams'

    b 'people living in Paris'?

3 Which text do you think is more interesting to read?

Building your skills

What you have been exploring is called hypernymy and hyponymy. It's the way we categorize the words we use. Here are some examples.

- Hypernym: colour
- Hyponyms: red, blue, yellow
- Synonyms of red: scarlet, blood-red, cherry, burgundy

Glossary

hypernym: the main word in a category, e.g. *traffic*

hyponym: specific examples within a category, e.g. *car* is a hyponym for *traffic*

1 Copy the grid below. Think of three to five synonyms for each of the hyponyms. The first one is done for you as an example.

HYPERNYM	Size		Emotions	
HYPONYMS	Large	Small	Scared	Happy
SYNONYMS	Big, massive, huge			

Developing your writing

Write a description of walking through a forest at night. Imagine that it is beginning to get dark and you can't quite remember your way home.

Describe what you see, hear and feel. Hypernyms and hyponyms might include trees and creatures that you notice and emotions that you feel. The idea is to produce a piece of writing with a range of words to avoid repetition. Aim to write 100 words.

Hints for Success

- Focus on using a range of words. Think about words which will describe the senses (sight, smell, taste, touch and sound).

Word Booster

Try to use some of the following words to make your description more interesting:

- Hyponyms for the hypernym of 'atmosphere': *gloomy*, *darkening*, *chilly*, *fading*

Choosing the Right Tense for Stories

Big Picture As we become more confident as writers, we use different tenses for different types of text. This unit explores how to use the **present** and **past tense** in stories and descriptions.

Skills ● Understand how and when to use present and past tenses.

Getting started

Here are some sentences in the present and past tenses.

PRESENT TENSE	PAST TENSE
I walk; I am walking	I walked; I have walked; I was walking; I was having to walk
She eats breakfast; she is eating breakfast	She ate breakfast; she was eating breakfast; she had eaten breakfast
He plays guitar; he is playing guitar	He played guitar; he was playing guitar; he had played guitar

> **Glossary**
>
> **past tense:** verbs which show an action takes place in the past, usually in the -ed form, e.g. *The hyena howled*.
>
> **present tense:** verbs which show an action takes place in the present, e.g. *The hyena howls*.

1 Now look at the list of different writing tasks you might be asked to complete in school. For each one decide whether you would write your response to the task in the present or past tense.

    a a story in English   **b** an evaluation in Science

    c a History essay   **d** a solution to a Maths problem

2 Compare your responses with a partner.

Building your skills

Now explore the different effects of using the present and past tenses in your writing. First, read these two versions of the same story – text A has been written in the past tense, whereas text B has been written in the present.

> **Text A: Past**
>
> As I walked into the classroom I sensed something was wrong. Everyone seemed to be looking at me. I panicked, wondering whether I'd forgotten to put on the right clothes or something. Why was everyone staring at me like that? These were people who knew me well, who were my friends, so why were they treating me in this way? Then Harry snorted with laughter. 'Surprise,' he said, and held out a massive cake with 'Happy Birthday' written on top.

Text B: Present

As I walk into the classroom I sense something is wrong. Everyone seems to be looking at me. I panic, wondering whether I have forgotten to put on the right clothes or something. Why is everyone staring at me like this? These are people who know me well, who are my friends, so why are they treating me in this way? Then Harry snorts with laughter. 'Surprise,' he says, and holds out a massive cake with 'Happy Birthday' written on top.

1   Write down three words that have changed tense in the texts.

2   Now look at the statements below. For each one, decide whether it describes text A, text B, both versions or neither.

    a Makes it seem more like a story   **b** Makes it seem like a joke

    c Makes it seem more immediate   **d** Makes it seem easy to follow

    e Makes it seem more formal   **f** Makes it seem more like a spoken text

Developing your writing

Write the opening of a story which details something that happened to you, such as a birthday you remember.

Write your story twice: once in the past tense, once in the present. Try to make each story no more than 50 words in length. Underneath, write a short paragraph saying what you found easy or difficult about the task and which version of the story you prefer.

Hints for Success

- Remember that the present tense and past tense can take different forms (*I eat/I am eating/I ate*).

- Pay close attention to the vocabulary you use: bring the scene to life through the careful use of synonyms.

Word Booster

Try to use some of the following words to make your opening more interesting:

- Adjectives: *excitable, childlike, spectacular*

- Adverbs: *hurriedly, excitedly, fantastically*

Choosing the Right Tense for Factual Writing

Big Picture On page 42 you looked at the differences between present and past tenses, and then at how to choose which one to use in descriptive or narrative writing. This unit looks at factual writing – essays, reports and evaluations.

Skills
- Be able to choose the correct tense for factual writing.

Getting started

Start by making sure you understand the difference between the past and present tenses.

1 Below are six sentences. For each one decide whether it has been written in a form of the present or past tense:

SENTENCE	PAST OR PRESENT?
The boat drifted slowly away along the shore.	
She sits in silent terror and hopes that she is wrong.	
He had hoped that this might never happen.	
Another day begins in bright hope.	
I am thinking of heading outside.	
There was no time like the present.	

2 Compare your answers with a partner. Which sentences did you find most difficult to decide on and why?

Building your skills

1 Here are some of the different types of factual writing you might be expected to do in school. For each one decide whether you would expect to use the past or present tense:

   a A report of an experiment in Science

   b A literature essay about a novel you have read in English

   c An evaluation for a product you designed in D&T

   d Instructions for a recipe in Food Technology

2 Now look at these examples of a student's factual writing for school.

   a Decide which tense is being used in each example (past or present).

   b Decide whether the student has selected the right tense for the task.

> **Scientific report**
>
> Water is added to the Petri dish. Heat is then applied. Bubbles begin to show. Boiling is starting.

English essay

Shakespeare's Macbeth was a hero at the start of the play but by the end he was a villain. When he first entered the play people greeted him as a brilliant warrior. He changed very quickly.

History essay

Mary Stuart is now known as Mary Queen of Scots. Born the daughter of James V of Scotland, she is famous for becoming Queen of Scotland.

Developing your writing

Based on your work on tenses in this unit, put together a fact-sheet for other students in your year group which:

a gives advice on recognizing past and present tenses

b gives advice on when to use the past and present tenses

c provides a sample of one type of factual writing to show students how to get the style right, annotated with arrows pointing to the verbs that are written in the present or past tense.

Hints for Success

- Work on your fact-sheet in a group. Each person could write about how to use tenses for a different text-type, which could make the basis for a useful display of how to write in different subjects.

- Remember that deciding which tense to use won't always be straightforward. Sometimes in History, for example, you may write about a famous figure in the past tense (*Winston Churchill was best known as Prime Minister…*) and at other times in the present tense (*His greatest achievement is leading Britain when…*).

Word Booster

Try to use some of the following words to make your fact-sheet more specific and informative:

- Verbs that are often used in specialist subjects: *evaluate*, *design*, *reflect*, *imagine*

Matching Your Language to Your Audience

Big Picture Effective writers always think about their **audience**. They think about what the audience wants when reading their work and then they try to create a text which is interesting, informative and entertaining for their readers.

Skills
- Understand who your audience is and match your language accordingly.

Getting started

When thinking about your audience, you may be tempted to sum it up in a fairly basic way, such as: older or younger people, female or male. This unit shows you ways of thinking about audience in a more specific way, which will make your language more precise.

Depending on the audience, the language style for your text can be either:
- informal or formal
- personal or impersonal
- general or specialist.

1 Read the description of what each language style means and when you are likely to use it. Then, for each one, think about how it would affect your choice of words.

	WHO IS YOUR AUDIENCE?		HOW WILL YOUR CHOICE OF WORDS BE AFFECTED?
INFORMAL OR FORMAL	If you know your audience well (e.g. if they are your friends), you might use more informal language, such as **contractions**.	If you don't know your audience personally, your language will often be more formal.	**a** How will your language be different if it is for an informal audience instead of a formal one? Think of an example.
PERSONAL OR IMPERSONAL	If you know your audience well (e.g. if they are your friends), you will want to use more personal language.	If you don't know your audience personally, your language will typically be more impersonal.	**b** How will your words be different using a personal, rather than impersonal, style? How will you refer to yourself or your reader differently?
GENERAL OR SPECIALIST	If your audience isn't knowledgeable about your subject, you will use more general language.	If your audience has knowledge of your subject, then your language can be more technical and specific.	**c** How will you choose language differently if you know that your audience has expert knowledge of the topic?

2 Compare your answers with a partner.

Glossary

audience: the group of people who will read a text

character: a person (and sometimes an animal) presented in a novel, play or film

contraction: a shortening of a word or words by dropping certain letters, e.g. the contracted form of *is not* is *isn't*; contractions are often used in informal speech and writing

Building your skills

Now look at these three texts based on the film series *Mission Impossible*.

1 Copy the grid below and, using a scale of 1 (low) to 5 (high), decide how formal, personal and general each text is. Use the third column to explain why you have given the rating.

Ghost Protocol, the fourth film in the *Mission Impossible* franchise, has now cumulatively taken more than $134 million in the USA, surpassing the final gross of *Mission: Impossible III* ($134 million).	Formal rating:	Reason:
	Personal rating:	Reason:
	General rating:	Reason:
Ghost Protocol is my favourite of the *Mission Impossible* films. I really like the way it combines special effects with strong characters and a dazzling storyline.	Formal rating:	Reason:
	Personal rating:	Reason:
	General rating:	Reason:
The original theme music from the television version of *Mission Impossible* was composed in 5/4 time. This was also used for Dave Brubeck's legendary jazz number, *Take Five* and in Gustav Holst's *Mars*.	Formal rating:	Reason:
	Personal rating	Reason:
	General rating:	Reason:

Developing your writing

Below are some facts about wasps. Write two short texts using this information.

Facts about wasps:

- medium-sized flying insects
- 75,000 recognized species
- on death they release a pheromone warning other wasps of danger
- live for 12–22 days
- 10,000 may inhabit one nest

1 Write the opening of a story for young children (aged under six), with a cute wasp as its main **character**. Make it informal and use simple vocabulary. Aim to write 100 words.

2 Write a 100-word opening of a fact-sheet about wasps, aimed at 13-year-old Science students. Make it impersonal and formal and use some specialist terms.

Hints for Success

- These are two contrasting texts; try to make them feel different.
- Use short sentences in the children's story.

Word Booster

Consider the audience for each of the texts; try to use some of the following words and techniques in your writing:

- Informal: use contractions and familiar words.
- Specialist: use technical terms, e.g. *pheromones*.
- Impersonal: avoid using *I*; use the passive voice.

Making Your Writing More Formal

Big Picture   A frequent criticism of students' answers in English exams is that their writing is too informal. To get the highest marks in most subjects – not just English – you need to be able to use a more formal style.

Skills   ● Learn ways of writing more formally.

Getting started   This is a piece of informal writing. Read it through and then use the questions which follow to explain what makes it informal.

> I've always been mad about go-karts. It's probably because we live up a hill and I've always dreamt of making a wooden go-kart that I could bomb down the hill on and terrify all the neighbours as I yelled 'Yee-ha!' like a character in a western. I know it's a daft idea but a go-kart would be a brilliant thing to make and if you found all the bits of wood and stuff lying around I don't think it would be that expensive.

1 Find five features of the text that shows you that it is written in an informal style.

2 Compare your ideas with a partner.

3 What advice would you give the writer to help them make their writing more formal?

Building your skills   Here are four suggestions for making your writing more formal:

Technique 1   Use Standard English words (words found in a dictionary rather than in a local dialect) and fewer **colloquial** words (words used in conversation). Instead of 'I've always been mad about go-karts', the writer could have used 'interested in', 'fascinated by', 'drawn to', etc.

Technique 2   Use fewer contracted forms. 'I have always been…' sounds more formal than 'I've always been…'.

Technique 3   Formal writing may use more **polysyllabic** words – words with more than one syllable. Instead of 'bomb' down the hill the writer could have chosen 'travel' or 'hurtle'; instead of 'mad about' she could have chosen 'passionate about'.

Technique 4   Use more varied sentences – some short, simple sentences and some using subordination. Informal writing may join clauses with 'and' and 'but', making longer sentences. The second sentence would become more formal and less chatty if it began like this: 'Living up a hill as a child was probably the cause of my fascination with go-karts…'

1   Using the four techniques, try rewriting the go-kart text in a more formal style.

> **Glossary**
>
> **colloquial:** informal words that would be used in conversation, e.g. saying *It's cool* when you mean something is good
>
> **connective:** a word that links phrases or sentences together, e.g. *and*, *or*, *before*, *later*
>
> **polysyllabic:** a word containing more than one syllable, e.g. *helicopter* contains four syllables: *hel-i-cop-ter*

Developing your writing

Practise writing in a more formal way, using the four techniques in this unit. Think back to your early experience of school – nursery, primary or secondary stage. Write 100 words in which you describe what you remember. Write it so that it is formal rather than chatty, but still tells your story clearly.

> **Hints for Success**
>
> - This is a tough assignment – it needs skill to get the tone right. You may decide that you want to keep some contracted forms in your writing (e.g. *I'd* rather than *I had*).
>
> - In particular, choose your words carefully so that they are precise and vivid. Don't choose complicated words just for the sake of it.
>
> **Word Booster**
>
> Try to use some of the following words to make your response more formal and interesting:
>
> - Sensuous adjectives: *nervous, shivering, panic-stricken, laughing, frowning, smiling, shaking, delicious*
>
> - **Connectives** other than just *and* and *but*: *however, although, as, when*

Using Informal Language in Your Writing

Big Picture   For most writing you do in school you will be expected to write in a formal way, using Standard English. However, there may be some occasions when you need your style to be more informal – for example, when you are including **dialogue** in your work and, therefore, want to use **slang** or dialect words.

Skills
- Understand the right contexts for informal language and how to use it.

Getting started

You won't often be asked by your teacher to make your writing more informal. Usually it will be the other way round – you will be required to be more formal.

However, there are some writing contexts where formal writing will seem odd. Look at this letter from an 11-year-old boy to his grandmother:

> Dear Grandmother,
>
> It is with the greatest appreciation that I find myself writing to you today. I wanted to put in writing my most fulsome thanks for the gift voucher that you dispatched to me to celebrate my recent birthday. It was quite charming of you, and is certainly much appreciated by me. I shall use it to purchase a game for my computer.
>
> Hearty thanks,
>
> Matt

1 This certainly feels ultra-formal for a number of reasons. Look at some of the words and phrases used in the grid below and decide what alternative words could be used to make the letter less formal.

FORMAL WORD OR PHRASE	CHANGE TO INFORMAL LANGUAGE
It is with the greatest appreciation	
my most fulsome thanks	
dispatched to me	
much appreciated by me	
I shall use it	
purchase	
Hearty thanks	

2 Which word or phrase did you have most difficulty finding an alternative for? Try to explain why.

Building your skills

Below are some suggestions to make your writing more informal.

In personal writing, letters and autobiographies:

Technique 1 Use more contracted forms: 'it's', not 'it is'; 'we've', not 'we have'.

Technique 2 Use more informal and colloquial vocabulary: 'great' instead of 'enjoyable'; 'big' instead of 'enormous'.

Technique 3 Use more coordination, by joining clauses with 'and' and 'but': 'We had a great time and I'm looking forward to going out and it should be brilliant fun…'

In dialogue (within stories, plays and autobiographies):

Technique 4 Use non-standard words from a local dialect: '"Stop bolting your food down like that!" shouted Mam.'

Technique 5 Show informal **pronunciation**: '"He don't wanna go. Leave him be," she said.'

1 Write a personal, informal letter or email to a friend or relative, using the advice above.

Developing your writing

Compose a piece of personal writing about an event in your own childhood. Include dialogue in which family or friends use informal language or dialect words. Choose one of the topics below:

- A family occasion to remember
- My earliest memory of a relative
- A time an argument broke out

Glossary

dialogue: speech in a novel, play or film

pronunciation: the way a word sounds when it is spoken

slang: informal words and phrases, which are often used in speech by a particular group of people

Hints for Success

- The aim here is to demonstrate that you can use informal language when appropriate. Try to use some of the techniques outlined above.

- As always with personal writing, aim to paint a picture in the reader's mind: make it vivid.

Word Booster

Try to use some of the following words and technique to make your response more formal:

- Contracted forms: *it's*, *I've*

- Personal pronouns: *I*, *me*, *she*, *us*

- Dialect words (*Mam*) and informal pronunciation (*innit?*)

Generating Ideas for Your Writing

Big Picture Quite often students, and even accomplished writers, struggle to think of ideas when they are given a writing task. This is the stage before actually writing anything, when you are generating ideas: it's called composition.

Skills • Learn techniques to help generate ideas for your writing.

Getting started

Start by analysing how well you currently come up with ideas.

1 Here is a list of possible tasks you could be given in an English lesson. For each one assess, on a scale of 1 (not confident) to 5 (confident), how well you feel you could come up with ideas for it.

TASK	RATING (1–5)
Write a story that uses techniques to build suspense.	
Write an analysis of a character in a novel you have read.	
Write a speech to persuade someone to agree with your views on a controversial topic (e.g. people who smoke should not receive free medical care).	
Write a descriptive piece about a key moment in your childhood.	
Write a letter to a politician suggesting a project that would help your neighbourhood.	

2 Now look at the task that you feel least confident with; why do you think you would find this task difficult? Is it because you don't understand the task, you don't know what language you should use or you understand the task but can't think how to start?

Building your skills

Here are a number of tips for generating ideas for your writing.

1 Think of books you have read and films you have seen. Try to recall different scenes, characters and events. Think of how they might be adapted for your writing. Create a spider diagram of characters, scenes and events that you would like to include in your writing.

2 Some writers say that once they have worked out their opening line or paragraph, the rest of the writing becomes easier. Try these different opening techniques:

   a Start with a question ('What was I doing there?').

   b Start with dialogue to immediately draw the reader in ('So it's time?' he asked. 'Yes, it's time,' I responded).

   c Start with a description of something in close detail ('The car's bonnet was battered and rusting. It had obviously been lying there in the wheat field for several weeks…').

   d Experiment with telling the story in the second person: 'You stepped from the house that morning and you suddenly felt cold, didn't you, as you noticed the mist gathered around your house. You set off slowly…'.

3 Use the 'hand-planning technique' – this helps you to generate five paragraphs for a topic. Look at the example below, which a student has used to plan their response to a descriptive writing task about a person they admire.

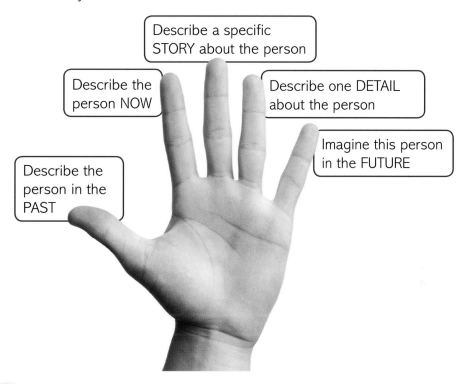

Describe a specific STORY about the person

Describe the person NOW

Describe one DETAIL about the person

Imagine this person in the FUTURE

Describe the person in the PAST

Developing your writing

Choose one of the writing tasks below. Use the techniques from the 'Building your skills' section to generate ideas for it. Then write either the opening sequence or the whole assignment.

- Write a story about a day that starts normally and then everything changes.
- Write a letter to your head teacher suggesting that the timings of the school day should be changed.
- Write a speech in which you persuade local councillors that they should get young people more involved in the community.

Hints for Success

- This unit is about planning, so put your energy into thinking of ideas, jotting them down and trying out new ones.

Word Booster

Try to use some of the following words in your response:

- Active verbs (*drifted, awakened, built*), vivid adjectives and adverbs (*smoky, disturbing, unfortunately*)

- Adverbials at the start of sentences (*Later that morning.../Another way of looking at it...*)

Using a Notebook to Improve Your Writing

Big Picture   Writing can be hard work. It often depends on our motivation – whether we are writing because we choose to or whether we are being required to write by someone else. Even professional writers sometimes struggle to write. This unit uses some of their advice – especially using a notebook to generate ideas.

Skills
- Explore how using a notebook could help you to develop new ideas and improve your writing.

Getting started   Read this advice by a range of writers on how to write successfully:

Anthony Horowitz

My advice is fairly simple. 1) The more you read, the better you'll write. 2) The more you write, the better you'll write. 3) Believe in yourself. It's not easy getting started and there'll always be someone to tell you you're not going to succeed. They're wrong. The only difference between a successful writer and an unsuccessful writer is that the unsuccessful writer gives up. 4) Have fun. You need something to write about so make sure you have plenty of experience. Travel. Meet people.

PD James

Increase your word power. Words are the raw material of our craft. The greater your vocabulary the more effective your writing. We who write in English are fortunate to have the richest and most versatile language in the world. Respect it.

Geoff Dyer

Keep a diary. The biggest regret of my writing life is that I have never kept a journal or a diary. Do it every day. Make a habit of putting your observations into words and gradually this will become instinct. This is the most important rule of all and, naturally, I don't follow it.

1 Which of the writers' tips do you find most helpful?

2 Think about your current attitude to writing.

   a What have you written out of school that you have enjoyed writing?

   b What have you written in school that you have enjoyed?

   c Where (in which room) do you write best?

   d How do you write best (computer, pen, pencil)?

3 On a scale of 1 (not very) to 5 (very), how difficult do you find the following writing tasks?

   a Coming up with new ideas

   b Knowing how to use language in an interesting way

   c Keeping focused and finishing your writing

4 Look back at your answers. In light of the authors' advice, what might you start to do to help develop your writing skills further?

Building your skills

Many writers say that writing is a practised discipline. It becomes easier if you do some writing every day in your own time. It is extremely useful to have a diary or journal in which to:

- note down things that have happened during the day
- write down funny observations about people
- say when you're pleased or angry about something
- note down any comments, quotations, statistics or other interesting items you have seen or heard.

1 Record what happened to you today in a notebook or journal. Aim to write 100 words. Remember to include your thoughts, feelings and any interesting or funny observations.

Developing your writing

Take a piece of plain paper and a pencil or pen and do some 'automatic writing' – write down any thoughts and ideas that come into your mind. It could be a description of the room you are in, your journey this morning or a memory from childhood, for example.

Hints for Success

- Finding ten minutes or so a day to do some writing is something lots of people do. In a busy world it can make us feel calm. Practise building it into your daily routine.

- You can write on a computer, but there will be distractions, such as the temptation to surf the Internet. A small notebook is the best journal.

Developing Original Ideas for Stories

Big Picture Many students know how to write well. What they struggle with is the process before the writing begins: with how to generate ideas for interesting and original stories. This unit will show you how to develop your creative writing.

Skills
- Practise techniques that will help you to write more interesting stories.

Getting started

Read these comments from three authors about how they get their initial ideas:

'Mostly it's a first line or an image or a vague sense of a situation.' – Bobbie Ann Mason

'All of my books come to me in the form of a sentence, an original sentence which contains the entire book.' – Raymond Federman

'I always begin with a character, or characters, and then try to think up as much action for them as possible.' – John Irving

Glossary

character: a person (and sometimes an animal) presented in a novel, play or film

dialogue: speech in a novel, play or film

noun: a thing, name or place, e.g. *panda*, *teacher*, *book*, *Ravi*, *London*

pronoun: a word that takes the place of a noun in a sentence, e.g. *it*, *that*, *he*

question: a sentence that asks for information or for a response and ends in a question mark, e.g. *Do you like ice cream?*

1 Try to stimulate some ideas for a story by doing some automatic writing. Concentrate on a blank page of paper. Use the ideas below to write something (it can be anything!). At this stage do not worry about the quality of what you are writing or where it may be heading.

- Think of a person, place, image or event that you remember from your childhood.
- Look at the sentence below. Write down what happens next.

  > The car reversed slowly until, with a sickening thud, it hit the wall.

- Write down some unexpected or dramatic **dialogue**. Think about who is saying it and why.

Building your skills

1 Different writers have different starting points for writing stories. Try these further writing exercises to stimulate more ideas.

  a Think of a **character**. Write down a name. Decide on where the character lives, what they look like, their age and where they are going.

  b Write an opening sentence which keeps the reader guessing about what is happening. Try to use **pronouns**, rather than **nouns**, so that the reader is not sure what is being referred to: 'She hadn't been here before.'

Glossary

connective: a word that links phrases or sentences together, e.g. *and*, *or*, *before*, *later*

viewpoint: the way a writer recounts a story, e.g. first person (*I…*), second person (*you…*) and third person (*she/he/they…*)

c Imagine the opening location of your story: sketch it in pictures or words. Write three key words to describe the location. Choose one detail (a door, the lawn, the dusty hall) and describe it further.

d Visualize a vivid image. Write it down, describing its colours, sounds, smells, tastes and textures.

e Think of some interesting dialogue. Make it surprising or unusual, so that the reader cannot understand it on its own.

f Look at the images below. Use one to kick-start your writing.

Developing your writing

Choose one of the ideas that have come out of the earlier exercises. Which one most captures your interest? Use it to start writing the opening of a story. Think about:

* the tense you will use – past or present
* the **viewpoint** – first person (I), second (you) or third (he/she/they)
* using interesting **connectives**
* adding variety by using statements, **questions** and dialogue.

Hints for Success

* Read. Almost all writers say that reading helps them to write their own stories.

* Use pronouns to keep your reader guessing. *She didn't recognize him* may grab a reader's attention more than immediately telling the names of characters.

Using Dialogue in Stories

Big Picture Some novels and short stories use lots of dialogue. It can help us to understand characters and their relationships better. However, it is important not to include too much, as this could become boring and may prevent the story moving forward. This unit will help you to get the balance right.

Skills
- Understand how to use dialogue effectively in a story.

Getting started

Below is an extract from a mystery story written by a Year 9 student.

'Any news?' said Will.

'No,' said Sarah.

'So what do you think has happened?' said Tom.

'It's too early to tell,' said Sarah.

'Have you called the police?' asked Tom.

'Of course,' said Sarah. 'They're on their way.'

1 What do you think of this piece of writing? Copy the grid below and use it to record your opinions about the dialogue.

STATEMENT	AGREE	UNSURE	DISAGREE
The dialogue grabs the reader's interest.			
The writer could use more interesting speech **verbs** than 'said'.			
The dialogue helps us to know what is happening in the story.			
The dialogue helps us to understand what the characters are like.			
The story would be more interesting with some description of the setting and characters.			

> **Glossary**
>
> **verb:** a word that tells you about the action in a sentence, e.g. *swam* is the verb in the following sentence: *The fish swam around the tank*.

2 What one piece of advice would you give to the student to improve their writing?

Building your skills

Now look at these two revised versions of the story. The first changes the speech verbs; the second adds in lots of description. Decide whether you think the text has been improved as a result of these changes.

Text A: Changing the speech verbs

'Any news?' asked Will.

'No,' replied Sarah.

'So what do you think has happened?' wondered Tom.

'It's too early to tell,' snapped Sarah.

'Have you called the police?' demanded Tom.

'Of course,' hissed Sarah. 'They're on their way.'

Text B: Adding detail

The garden was still. 'Any news?' said Will.

'No,' said Sarah, looking at her phone. A rook in a distant tree screeched.

'So what do you think has happened?' said Tom. He looked white-faced.

'It's too early to tell,' said Sarah, her lip trembling.

'Have you called the police?' asked Tom. He hated asking all these questions but couldn't stop himself.

'Of course,' said Sarah. 'They're on their way.' There was silence. Tom looked at his watch nervously.

1 Take each text in turn, and answer the following:

a What changes do you notice between the original text and this version?

b Do you think this version is better than the original? Why or why not?

Developing your writing

Imagine two friends talking. One is very stressed about exams; the other is trying to tell a very important secret. Tell the story through dialogue, thinking carefully about the speech verbs you use and adding descriptive detail when appropriate.

Hints for Success

● The writer David Almond believes that 'said' or 'asked' is usually the best speech verb. Use other speech verbs only when they help readers to understand the character or situation better.

Word Booster

Try to use some of the following words in your dialogue:

● Alternative speech verbs: *suggested, muttered, whispered*

● Descriptive adverbs: *softly, aggressively, jokingly*; and adjectives: *worried, frustrated*

Using Telling and Showing to Create Characters

Big Picture Stories are almost always based around characters. Usually these are humans, although occasionally they may be animals or insects, as in children's books. Once you have settled on which characters you will include in your story, you need to then consider how best to bring them to life.

Skills
- Explore different techniques for creating memorable characters.

Getting started Look at these two descriptions of a character. What is the writer doing differently in each one?

Text A

> He was a bad-tempered man and I used to avoid him. He would bark out instructions and generally treat me as if he hated me. He always had jobs for me to do.

Text B

> 'Hurry up,' he barked. His eyes drilled into mine. 'Come on, we haven't got all day'. He had found me hiding away in the kitchen. Now he stood there, broom in his hand, waiting for me to get started on another list of jobs. My stomach tightened in a knot as I reached out and took the broom.

1 In text A what do we learn about the man and the narrator ('I')?

2 What do we learn about them both in text B?

3 What does text A tell you that text B doesn't?

4 What does text B tell you that text A doesn't?

5 Which version do you prefer and why?

Building your skills Writers know that sometimes they need to tell their readers information directly about a character ('He was a bad-tempered man') but, at times, they may want their readers to work out information for themselves ('Hurry up,' he barked).

This is the difference between telling and showing. Telling can be quicker because it needs fewer words; showing usually requires more words. Telling is used more in children's stories; for example: 'The giant was unhappy.'

1 Look at the grid at the top of page 61, which includes three examples of showing and two of telling. For each example of *showing*, write down what the writer is *telling* us about the character. For each example of *telling*, think of how it could be written to *show* the character traits.

SHOWING	TELLING
He slammed his hand down on the desk and looked around him.	He was…
The laughter filled the playground as the children ran around.	They were…
As she listened to her daughter's account, her eyes narrowed and her smile faded.	She was…
	She was nervous.
	He was hungry.

Developing your writing

Practise your showing and telling skills. Imagine a student is in trouble and has been sent to the office of a senior teacher in a school. He or she is standing outside the office. On the surface the student seems confident, but inside they are terrified of what is about to happen.

Write a description of the scene in which you:

- tell the reader what your character looks like, what they are wearing and where they are standing
- show the reader how your character is feeling (by describing their eyes and facial expression, how they are standing, small hints of nervousness, and so on).

Hints for Success

- Remember: this is a writing exercise. You'll need to practise and change words as you develop your skills. Don't expect your first version to be right straight away.

Word Booster

Try to use some of the following words to make your description more interesting:

- Verbs which describe bodily movements: *flickered*, *narrowed*, *frowned*, *glanced*

- Adjectives and adverbs (used occasionally) to add details: *cold*, *empty*, *furious*; *slowly*, *deliberately*, *uncontrollably*

Using Description in Stories

Big Picture   Description in stories helps readers to visualize characters and setting. The problem is that too much description bores us, whereas too little description leaves us not feeling engaged with the story.

Skills
- Know how to achieve the right balance of description in stories.

Getting started

Read this Year 8 student's story opening:

> The sun was beating down from the bright blue sky over the yellow sandy beach where the many bathers were lying on the baking sand. Overhead a large group of noisy gulls were making loud screeching sounds and looking for delicious food.

1 What do you like about the text?

2 What do you dislike about it?

3 What two pieces of advice would you give to the student to help her improve the description?

Building your skills

We can add detail to our writing in a number of ways:
- choosing verbs that more vividly describe what is happening
- pre-modification – adding an **adjective** in front of a noun: 'the *vibrant sunset*'
- post-modification – adding a phrase or **clause** after a noun: 'The sunset, *which was vibrant…*'
- adding **adverbs** to make verbs more descriptive: 'The sun was *slowly* setting.'

Read these three paragraphs of description. Which do you think achieves the best balance between too much and too little description?

Text A

The clock struck nine. It was later than I had realized. A car pulled up and I got in.

Text B

The ancient grandfather clock struck nine with a loud and rhythmic thump. With a terrifying squeal of brakes, a car suddenly pulled up alongside the no parking sign outside our house. I pulled open the door, jumped in and off we sped.

Text C

The ancient grandfather clock, which had been a present from a member of my mother's family some thirty years ago, struck nine o'clock, making us all jump. Suddenly and unexpectedly the silence was shattered by a terrifyingly loud squeal of brakes, as my uncle's old Citroen rammed into the edge of the pavement by our house. 'Hey up,' shouted Uncle Joe with a hearty laugh. I jumped quickly in, slammed the door behind me and off we sped.

1 For each text, write down one thing you like and one thing you dislike.

2 Which text do you think works best overall?

3 If you were giving someone advice on how to use description in their writing, what would it be?

Developing your writing

Here is some rather dull writing. Rewrite it using some more descriptive language so that it is more interesting.

Captain Fawcett got into the cockpit and started to check the controls. He saw that everything seemed OK. His co-pilot was with him. They waited till all the passengers were on board and then they waited for clearance to take off. They did not realize that there was a passenger on board who was about to get very ill.

How will you help readers to feel part of the scene? How will you paint a picture of the cockpit and of the sick passenger?

Glossary

adjective: a describing word used to give more information about a noun, e.g. *The beautiful diamond sparkled magnificently.*

adverb: a word which gives more information about how an action is carried out, e.g. *The beautiful diamond sparkled magnificently.* Adverbs often end in -ly.

clause: a group of words which includes a subject and a verb, e.g. *When I run in the evening*

Hints for Success

- Select powerful verbs, and adjectives and adverbs which appeal to the senses.
- Use dialogue to bring your scene to life.

Using Literary Devices to Improve Your Writing

Big Picture One of the ways that writers make their texts more vivid and powerful is by using a range of special literary devices; these include **metaphors**, **similes** and **personification**. It's easy to think that these devices are only used in poems and stories but they are an essential part of a writer's toolkit for non-fiction too. This unit explores how to use them.

Skills ● Make your writing more vivid using literary devices.

Getting started

Used with care (i.e. not too often), literary devices can improve the quality of your storytelling and make your writing more interesting and engaging for your readers.

Metaphor The Greek word 'metaphor' means to move or transfer. Writers use metaphors to compare one thing with another – in fact we all do it all the time; for example, a brilliant football player might be described using these metaphors:

> He displayed the footwork of a ballet dancer.

> His legs were rubber after the performance.

These are examples of metaphor – comparing one thing (a football player) with another. Metaphors make comparisons by saying that one thing is another thing.

Simile Similes also compare one thing with another, but they more clearly tell the reader that they are comparing two different items by using the words 'like' or 'as'.

For example, a description of a netball game might include these similes:

> She remained as cool *as* a cucumber.

> The crowd were baying for a goal *like* animals.

Personification Personification takes things that are not alive (the weather, objects, concepts) and describes them as if they were. It can be a powerful way of creating fear or bringing a situation more fully to life:

> The wind rampaged across the back garden.

> The moon looked down from the darkening sky.

Building your skills

1 Imagine someone who is lost in the woods on a night when the light is fading and a storm is brewing. Write a paragraph in which you practise using metaphor, simile and personification. Use these ideas to help you:

- As I looked about, the forest…
- The cold air began to…
- The darkness started to…
- Like a…, the night began to…

2 Compare what you have written with a partner. Discuss ways in which you could improve your writing. Work with each other to make sure you are clear on the differences between the literary devices.

Developing your writing

Write the opening of a story in which someone is drifting in a boat at sea. Describe the weather, the atmosphere and the emotions of the person. Use some metaphors, similes and personification – but be careful not to do this in every sentence as it may be too intense.

You might start your description with: 'The small boat was drifting towards the horizon like…'

Glossary

metaphor: a literary device which compares two things by saying that one thing is another, e.g. *He was the apple of her eye.*

personification: a literary device which takes things that are not alive and describes them as if they are, e.g. *The wind scratched at the door.*

simile: a literary device which compares two things, using the words *like* or *as*, e.g. *Her hair was golden like the sun.*

Hints for Success

- Use language which helps the reader to visualize what is happening: imagine it as a film.

Word Booster

Try to use some of the following words in your story opening:

- Adjectives that appeal to the reader's senses: *dark, yellowing, bright, burnt, unpleasant, bitter, rough, jagged, warm*

Making Settings Seem Real in Stories

Big Picture   The best stories usually make us feel like we are in a real place with real people; the writer draws us into the world of their fiction. This unit shows you how to make **settings** come alive in your writing.

Skills
- Practise creating a powerful sense of place in your stories.

Getting started   Read this story opening and think about how well it creates a sense of place.

> I was in my car and I was driving through the countryside looking for a place called the White House. I kept looking around me but I couldn't see anything and it was starting to get darker. I began to worry that I might never arrive in time.

Glossary

setting: location of a novel, play or film

tension: the way writers hold back information to keep readers guessing what will happen next; also known as **suspense**

vocabulary: the range of words known by a person

1 What do you think? Does this piece of descriptive writing have the right level of detail to make the setting feel real? Why or why not?

2 Do you agree or disagree with the following statements?

   a The writing helps you to view the scene.

   b The choice of **vocabulary** is vivid.

   c There is the right level of descriptive writing.

   d The character seems real.

3 If you were giving the writer advice on how to improve their opening, what would it be?

Building your skills

Read the following extract from the opening of *The Small Hand* by Susan Hill. Consider how Susan Hill creates a sense of place in her writing.

> It was a little before nine o'clock, the sun was setting into a bank of smoky violet cloud and I had lost my way [...]
>
> The road had cut through the Downs, pale mounds on either side, and then run into a straight, tree-lined stretch to the crossroads. The fingerpost markings were faded and there were no recent signs. So that when the right turning came I almost shot past it, for there was no sign at all here, just a lane and high banks in which the roots of trees were set deep as ancient teeth. But I thought that this would eventually lead me back to the A road.

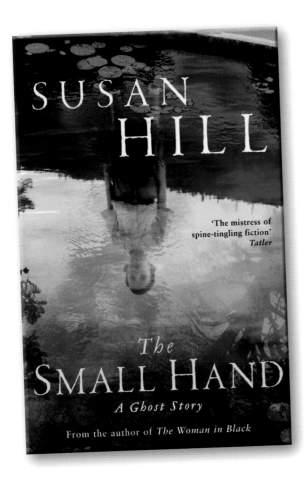

'The mistress of spine-tingling fiction'
Tatler

> The lane narrowed. The sun was behind me, flaring into the rear-view mirror. Then came a sharp bend, the lane turned into a single track and the view ahead was dark beneath overhanging branches […]
>
> I got out. Opposite me was an old sign, almost greened over. THE WHITE HOUSE. Below, someone had tacked up a piece of board. It hung loose but I could just make out the words GARDEN CLOSED in roughly painted lettering.

1 Draw a rough sketch in which you show the scene – the roads that the car travels on, the sign for THE WHITE HOUSE, etc.

2 How easy was it to draw the scene? Which parts of the writing were easiest to visualize and which were most difficult?

3 Write down three words that Susan Hill uses in her opening which help the reader to visualize the scene.

4 Which part of the description do you like most and why?

Developing your writing

Write a description of getting lost. Imagine you are on a walk with a friend. You have an argument and your friend runs off, leaving you alone. It is getting darker and you aren't sure of the route back. Describe the scene in a way that makes the reader visualize it. Try to build a sense of **tension**.

Hints for Success

- Write in the first person voice, using 'I'.

- Use vivid description.

- You might wish to include dialogue to establish the relationship between you and your friend on the walk.

Word Booster

Try to use some of the following words in your description:

- Words which paint a powerful picture: *darkening, isolated, mist*

- Active verbs: *crunched, barked, howled*

Using Different Viewpoints

Big Picture   In films, the camera constantly switches from one scene, and one set of characters, to another. Many writers do the same thing; to make their stories more interesting they change viewpoints – telling different parts of the story through the eyes of different characters.

Skills   • Learn how to use different viewpoints in a story.

Getting started   Here's the opening of a story written in three different ways, by changing the pronoun from 'I' to 'he' to 'you'.

Text A

I was surprised to see the old man at the back of the shop. I thought he had gone somewhere – left the area. I wondered whether to go up to him and say hello or whether to pretend I had not seen him.

Text B

James was surprised to see the old man at the back of the shop. He thought he had gone somewhere – left the area. He wondered whether to go up to him and say hello or whether to pretend he had not seen him.

Text C

You were surprised to see the old man at the back of the shop. You thought he had gone somewhere – left the area. You wondered whether to go up to him and say hello or whether to pretend you had not seen him.

Glossary

suspense: the way writers hold back information to keep readers guessing what will happen next; also known as **tension**

synonym: a word with a similar meaning to another word, e.g. *large* and *bulky* are synonyms of *big*

1   Which version of the story feels:

   a   most chatty

   b   most formal

   c   most sinister or disturbing

   d   most odd or unnatural?

2   Which version would you most want to continue reading? Why?

3   Choose one of the story openings. What advice would you give to the writer to make it more interesting?

Building your skills

Viewpoints in stories are usually in:

- the first person (written through the eyes of a main character using the pronoun 'I')
- the third person (the author describes the main character from the outside using the pronouns 'he', 'she' or 'they')

or

- the second person (using the pronoun 'you', though this is much more unusual).

Some writers add interest to their fiction by using different viewpoints within the same story. Look at the following example, based on *Little Red Riding Hood*, and notice how **suspense** can be added to a story when viewpoints are changed.

PARAGRAPH	VIEWPOINT	EXAMPLE
Paragraph 1	Third person, describing Little Red Riding Hood from the outside	'In a small cottage at the edge of the forest, a young girl skipped downstairs, pulling her red cape tighter around her shoulders. She knew it was going to be cold outside…'
Paragraph 2	Second person, describing Little Red Riding Hood as if the wolf is speaking	'You didn't see me, did you? You were too busy getting ready to leave the house. You called goodbye to your mother…'
Paragraph 3	First person, describing the thoughts of the woodcutter	'It was a normal Saturday morning and I knew I had some work to finish off. I grabbed my sandwiches and my chainsaw and headed out into the forest…'

Developing your writing

Either continue the *Little Red Riding Hood* story, using three different viewpoints, or write a similar story based on a fairy tale that you are familiar with. Remember to switch between first-, second- and third-person viewpoints.

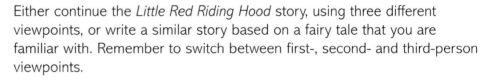

Hints for Success

- As with all writing, some ideas will work and some won't. Be critical and don't be afraid to change words and sentences.
- Use descriptive words to paint a picture of the setting.

Word Booster

Try to use some of the following words in your story:

- **Synonyms** to describe walking through the forest: *strolled, hurried, rushed, skipped*
- **Adjectives** to make the forest seem sinister: *misty, chilly, unnerving*

Writing Powerful Story Openings

Big Picture All writers know that you need to hook your reader's attention from the very beginning and keep them reading to the end. The novelist Brian Moore once said that he writes and rewrites the opening sequence of his novels dozens of times until he feels it is right. He said that, once he got the beginning right, the rest of the novel would flow more easily.

Skills
- Experiment with different techniques to make your opening interesting.

Getting started

Here are six ideas for starting a story in an interesting way, followed by examples from established writers.

TECHNIQUE	EXAMPLE
Dialogue	'Take my camel, dear,' said my Aunt Dot, as she climbed down from the animal on her return from High Mass. (Rose Macaulay, *The Towers of Trebizond*)
Starting in the middle of some action	Through the fence, between the curling flower spaces, I could see them hitting. (William Faulkner, *The Sound and the Fury*)
Description	The sky above the port was the colour of television, tuned to a dead channel. (William Gibson, *Neuromancer*)
Direct storytelling	I was born in the Year 1632, in the City of York, of a good Family, tho' not of that Country... (Daniel Defoe, *Robinson Crusoe*)
Direct introduction to a character	There was a boy called Eustace Clarence Scrubb, and he almost deserved it. (CS Lewis, *The Voyage of the Dawn Treader*)
First-person narration	I am an invisible man. (Ralph Ellison, *Invisible Man*)

1 Which of the techniques grabs your interest most?

2 Which technique do you think is the least effective or engaging?

Building your skills

The writer Michael Baldwin says that your opening sentence should contain one or more of these elements:

- an event
- a setting
- an idea.

1 In your school library, look at a sample of five novels and short stories and compare their opening sentences. Write down whether the openings include an event, a setting, an idea or a mixture of these elements. Decide which opening you think best makes the reader want to read on.

2 Look at the following dull story openings. For each one, using a technique from the grid on page 70, rewrite them in a more interesting way.

> I didn't like the look of the empty car park as I walked towards it that night.

> Daljeet saw the boat out of the corner of his eye and decided that it was travelling very quickly.

> 'Hello,' said the woman in the blue coat as she walked out of the carpet shop.

Developing your writing

Write the opening of a short story. It could be set in a disused school, a playground or a supermarket car park, for example. Choose a central character: a businessman, an old lady, a student on a bike or someone else. Then decide on a style for your opening: dialogue, mid-action, description or first-person narration, for example.

Make your opening as interesting as you can so that your reader will be keen to continue.

Hints for Success

- Try out different ideas and approaches before you settle on your favourite story opening.

- Remember that the best writing is usually vivid, helping us to see, hear, smell and almost touch the scene being described.

Word Booster

Try to use some of the following words and techniques to make your opening more interesting:

- Use vivid verbs, adjectives and adverbs.

- Avoid *he was/she was/it was* if possible.

Building Tension in Stories

Big Picture   Many people enjoy thrillers – films that keep us watching, and books that keep us turning the page to find out what happens next. Writers who achieve the right level of tension know just how much information to give the reader and how much to hold back.

Skills
- Learn how to build tension in writing.

Getting started

This unit explores four approaches to building tension:

- creating **atmosphere**
- using pronouns carefully
- delaying action
- varying sentence types.

Glossary

atmosphere: tone or mood

Look at these story extracts, written by Year 9 students, based on the legend of Theseus and the Minotaur. Which text makes you most want to read on?

Text A

It was there, lurking behind me. I couldn't see it, but I could feel it, its hot breath roasting my neck. I knew now was my last chance. I had no choice but to head deeper into the cave.

Text B

A heartbeat – that was all I heard. Was it mine or was it the creature's? He was following me now. This was just as I had planned it, but I knew that he knew his way around the cave better than I did.

Text C

It got darker and gloomier the further Theseus went into the cave. The hot sand under his feet had now turned cool and damp. The last flickers of daylight were behind him. He squinted, knowing that the creature was in here somewhere.

1 For each text, write down:

  a one word, phrase or idea that you like

  b one way the writer could improve their text. Try to make your suggestion as specific as possible, for example, a word that could be replaced by a better choice.

2 Give each text a tension rating, from 1 (low) to 5 (high).

3 What do you notice about the techniques each writer has used to try to build tension? How do the texts differ?

Building your skills

Explore these four common techniques for building tension.

Technique 1: Creating atmosphere

Choose words which help the reader to see, feel, hear and smell the scene.

LOW TENSION	HIGH TENSION
The yard was empty and there was no one there. Then a shadow moved.	A distant cat shrieked. Litter blew across the empty yard. Someone, or something, was moving in the dark shadows.

Technique 2: Delaying action

When your reader is expecting the next step during a tense moment in the story, put in a line of vivid description instead.

> Rachel knew this was the moment when she had to prove herself. Her heart thumping, she pulled open the door. *Outside, the sky remained a brilliant blue. A seagull squawked loudly.*

Technique 3: Choose your pronouns carefully

Pronouns – like 'he', 'she', 'they', 'it' – can be used to keep the reader guessing. The sentence 'He looked at it more closely' makes the reader work harder than 'The boy looked at the watch more closely': we start to predict who 'he' and 'it' might be.

Technique 4: Use some short sentences

Short sentences can build a rhythm in your writing, especially when placed alongside longer sentences.

> She carried on walking. Something was behind her. She paused. It paused. She realized that she had two choices: turn around or run.

Developing your writing

Practise building tension using the techniques above. Write a 100-word paragraph based on the following scenario:

You are at home on your own. It is getting dark outside. You hear the back door open. You head to the kitchen to investigate…

Hints for Success

- Use language that appeals to the senses.
- Practise using the techniques above: be experimental.

Word Booster

Try to use some of the following words to build suspense:

- Vivid verbs: *banged, creaked, thumped*
- Expressive adverbs: *noisily, carelessly, nervously*
- Powerful adjectives: *anxious, cautious, tentative*

Writing Powerful Story Endings

Big Picture   The more we read of a short story or novel, the faster our reading often becomes, because we are keen to find out how the story will unfold. However, we often slow down as we approach the end of a book because we want to take in more carefully what happens. Some endings surprise us; some are what we expected; some disappoint. This unit shows you how to improve your story endings.

Skills
- Explore different techniques for ending stories.

Getting started

Read the following story endings.

> Then she woke up and found that it had all been a dream.

> 'And so,' he said, 'I then decided that I wouldn't bother.'

> The door closed behind him forever.

> In that moment, she knew that life could never be the same again.

Glossary

cliff-hanger: a suspenseful ending to a novel or film

genre: type of story, e.g. *horror, romance, crime fiction*

1 Which story ending grabs your interest most?

2 What do you think each story was about and what **genre** (type of story) do you think it belongs to?

3 Which story ending do you think is the weakest? Why?

Building your skills

Here are some techniques for adding interest to your endings.

Technique 1: Atmospheric description   Shift the focus away from your character to the weather or the landscape. Think about how a film director might pull back the camera shot to show an actor looking smaller in a scene.

> 'Possibly,' Eleanor replied, peering towards the horizon. 'Just possibly.' The rain that had been threatening all day chose that moment to visit. She sat in the middle of the field, looking up, as the storm began its work.

Technique 2: Cliff-hanger   Surprise the reader with a sudden twist in the tale by using a **cliff-hanger**.

> Safe at last, she pulled the door behind her and switched on the light. As her gaze adjusted to the brightness she realized with a sickening feeling how wrong she was. Her old friend was back.

Technique 3: Dialogue   Use dialogue to hint at what the future holds for your characters.

> 'It's the only way,' he said. 'You have to do it.'
>   She looked him in the eyes and noticed the tears. 'OK. We'll see. Now let's go.'

Technique 4: Inconclusive endings   Inconclusive endings can frustrate readers, but will leave them guessing about what may happen next.

> He guessed that something would turn up. He just didn't know when. He waved a feeble hand, reached for his keys and climbed slowly into the car.

1 Review the techniques:

   a Which of these do you like most?

   b Which stories can you think of which have an ending like any of these?

Developing your writing

Here's an idea for a short story. Practise using the techniques from this unit to come up with some alternative endings for it. A boy and his family move into a new house. One day when the boy's parents are out he ventures up to the old attic because he thinks he has heard movement.

Describe the boy heading upstairs into the attic and what he sees. Experiment with telling the final part of the story and trying out the different endings.

Hints for Success

- Remember that this is a writing practice task: the aim is to try out different ideas and then to see which you think works best.

Word Booster

Try to use some of the following words in your ending:

- Powerful descriptive vocabulary: *darkening, fading, vanishing*

Making Chronological Stories More Interesting

Big Picture We generally tell stories in the order that the events happen. However, the problem is that this can sometimes be quite boring. This unit explores ways of making your **chronological** stories more interesting.

Skills
● Explore and practise techniques for making chronological stories exciting.

Getting started

How would you improve this piece of personal writing by a Year 7 student?

> My earliest memory is going to the theme park with my grandma. It was a hot day in July and we travelled in her car. We had to wait for something like 45 minutes in the queue outside the park. Then we finally got in and my grandma asked me what I wanted to go on. So I went to the map and looked at the different rides and then I remember it all being a bit confusing.

1 How interesting do you find the story, on a scale of 1 (not interesting) to 5 (very interesting)?

2 Choose three words that you would change in this text.

3 Which of the suggestions below do you think would most improve the story?

> A *Use short sentences.*
>
> B *Use a mix of short and long sentences.*
>
> C *Connect ideas with words other than 'and', 'so' and 'then'.*
>
> D *Tell the story in a different order.*

Glossary

chronological: in the order in which the events happened, starting with the earliest event

discourse marker: words or phrases used to signal a topic change or time-shift, e.g. *before*, *alternatively*

Building your skills

You can make chronological writing more interesting by cutting from one scene to another in your story, like this:

> Aamina sat in the back of the car, lost in the music from her earphones. She watched the countryside speeding past. She allowed herself to drift in and out of concentration and relaxed into the journey she had dreaded so much.
>
> The gates of the villa weren't what she had expected. The car slowed as they approached.

1 Look at the techniques the writer has used.

    a How do you know it will be a long journey?

    b How does the scene change at the start of the second paragraph?

    c How does the writer make their writing seem visual, like a film?

    d What is the effect of using 'she' in the second paragraph rather than repeating Aamina's name?

Sometimes you will want to signal how time has changed in your story when you switch scenes. You can use **discourse markers** to signal a time-shift, like these:

While	Later	Once	After	Earlier	Meanwhile	Some time later

2 What do you think are the advantages and disadvantages of using discourse markers in a story?

3 Comment on how the text feels different when told like this:

> Aamina sat in the back of the car...
>
>   Some time later, they approached the gates of the villa...

4 Which version do you prefer – with or without a discourse marker?

Developing your writing

Tell the story of yesterday's events in a series of short paragraphs, starting with getting up.

- Describe the events in the third person ('Late again, she ran to the bus stop').
- Start some paragraphs by simply cutting to the next scene.
- Start others using discourse markers.

Hints for Success

- Be experimental – sometimes cutting from one scene to the next may leave your reader too confused and a discourse marker may be clearer.

Word Booster

Try to use some of the following words in your response:

- Descriptive phrases: *grimy windows, growl of traffic, jarring bells*
- Discourse markers: *ten minutes later, soon after*

Writing Stories for Young Children

Big Picture The stories we read in early childhood are important. They feed our imaginations and help us to become better readers. A good children's story stays with us for life. So how do writers create them and how could you write a successful children's story?

Skills
● Identify the features in a good children's story and practise using them.

Getting started Here's a list of ten of the best-known stories aimed at young children.

1 How many of them do you know – either through reading the stories as a child or seeing film versions?

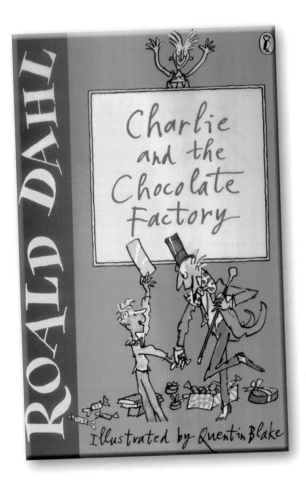

> *Goodnight Moon*: Margaret Wise Brown and Clement Hurd
>
> *Where The Wild Things Are*: Maurice Sendak
>
> *Gorilla*: Anthony Browne
>
> *Charlie and the Chocolate Factory*: Roald Dahl
>
> *The Legend of Captain Crow's Teeth*: Eoin Colfer
>
> *The Adventures of Captain Underpants*: Dav Pilkey
>
> *The Adventures of the Dish and the Spoon*: Mini Grey
>
> *Flat Stanley*: Jeff Brown
>
> *Ug: Boy Genius of the Stone Age*: Raymond Briggs
>
> *The Iron Man*: Ted Hughes

2 Is there one children's story that was special to you when you were young, but which isn't on the list? Create a spider diagram for the book, which includes information about:

● the author's name
● what the cover looked like
● names of characters
● what happened
● what you remember about reading it (when, where, with whom?)
● why it was so memorable.

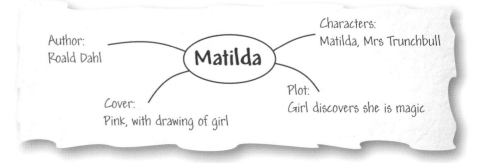

Author: Roald Dahl

Characters: Matilda, Mrs Trunchbull

Matilda

Cover: Pink, with drawing of girl

Plot: Girl discovers she is magic

Building your skills

A good children's story should contain:

- a strong straightforward **plot**
- a small number of characters (possibly animals or insects)
- interesting pictures that help the young reader to understand the story.

If you were to write a children's story, what would it be about? Here are some tips that will help you to generate ideas for your writing.

Glossary

alliteration: repetition of the first sound in two or more words or phrases, e.g. *the wild winds of winter*

plot: events placed in a pattern to tell a story

Tips for writing children's stories:

- Come up with a story that you can summarize in one sentence – e.g. 'A caterpillar eats lots of food and finally turns into a beautiful butterfly.'
- Stories rely on some kind of conflict – people disagreeing or things going wrong. In children's stories, the conflict usually ends happily.
- Choose a main character who is proactive and does things, rather than just reacts to other people's actions.

1 Think of a children's story you used to enjoy reading. Sum up its storyline in just one sentence.

Developing your writing

Choose a creature from the list below. They have been deliberately chosen because they create a challenge!

Rat	Locust	Snake	Mosquito

Decide on a name and think of your character's personality; remember that names of characters in children's entertainment often use **alliteration**, for example, Bob the Builder and Postman Pat.

Then write a short story that you could read to a pupil at a neighbouring primary school. Use the hints in this unit to guide you. Don't worry too much about the images; instead focus on making your character and story memorable and your language simple.

Hints for Success

- Think of the conflict at the heart of your story first.
- Keep the story moving, rather than giving too much description: this will keep your readers interested.
- Use words and phrases that are easy to understand, especially connectives that help to structure the story: *There was once… He decided… Later that day…*

Writing a Film or TV Script

Big Picture Writing a script for film or TV is different from writing a short story or novel; your work will be interpreted and possibly changed by other people – producers, the director and actors. Your role, therefore, is to give a really strong idea of how you think the story should be on-screen, but then to hand over the creative task to other people.

Skills
- Understand how film writers work and practise writing a script of your own.

Getting started

A script outlines what the writer expects the audience to see on-screen – the characters, the setting and the action. Notice the word: 'outlines'; however good you are as a scriptwriter, your work will be taken on by someone else to create the final film.

1 Think of three films you like. For each film, decide whether you agree or disagree with the following statements.

   a The film has a strong character that I identified with.

   b The main character faces obstacles.

   c The film has a 'What if…?' situation that grabbed my interest, taking me to a place or situation that was unfamiliar.

2 Which is your favourite film and why?

Building your skills

The way you set out your script is important. Here's what one expert says:

> Screenplays are traditionally written on 8$\frac{1}{2}$" x 11" white 3-hole punched paper. A page number appears in the upper right-hand corner (in the header). No page number is printed on the first page. The type style used is the Courier 12 font.
>
> The Courier 12 font is used for timing purposes. One script page in Courier 12 roughly averages 1 minute of on-screen film time. Experienced readers can detect a long script by merely weighing the stack of paper in their hand.

Read the opening of a script on page 81. Look at the way the writer tells the story.

1 What do you notice about the amount of stage directions in this opening sequence?

Glossary

past tense: verbs which show an action has taken place in the past, usually in the -ed form, e.g. *The hyena howled.*

present tense: verbs which show an action takes place in the present, e.g. *The hyena howls.*

```
DARKNESS. THE SOUND OF FIERCE WAVES.

MUSIC. TITLES.

EXT. OCEAN - NIGHT

The light from a distant LIGHTHOUSE flickers across
the screen. We see a BOAT. It appears empty. As the
CAMERA moves in, we detect a FACE, eyes closed. The
light catches the look of someone who appears in a
deep sleep in THICK CLOTHES AND HAT.

Suddenly another human moves into shot - another
FISHERMAN. He growls.


                   SAILOR #1

Typical. You ask me on a fishing trip, then you fall
asleep. Some special party this is proving. We've
been here hours and not seen a thing -


                   SAILOR #2

Huh? (STIRRING; OPENS EYES) Sorry, Dan, it's been a
long day, a really long day -


                   SAILOR #1

Yeah yeah, tell me about it -


The CAMERA moves to the edge of the BOAT. Something
is moving in the WATER but we can't yet tell what.
```

Developing your writing

Take a story you know well – for example, a nursery rhyme (*Humpty Dumpty*) or a Shakespeare play (*Macbeth*). Write the opening two scenes of a film version. Aim to introduce the main character and some conflict, so that the viewer wants to keep watching.

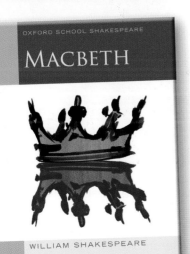

Hints for Success

- Remember that the story will be on-screen: this task is different from writing a story for a book.

- Keep your screen directions and instructions as brief as possible. Your focus should be on the story.

- Write character names in capitals.

- Write instructions and stage directions in the **present tense** (e.g. *The car moves slowly* rather than the **past tense** *The car moved slowly*).

Writing Science Fiction

Big Picture
Science fiction and fantasy writers often use unusual settings to tell their stories. The action might be set in the distant future or distant past or on planets many light-years from Earth. Some of the most interesting stories use settings that are unusual and yet familiar, so that the readers are not quite sure where or when the story is set.

Skills
- Explore some of the techniques used by science fiction and fantasy writers.

Getting started
Science fiction writers try to get us to see the world differently. Science fiction novels often start with a surprising opening sentence, which throws the reader into an unusual world or scenario. Here are five examples. Which opening line grabs your interest the most?

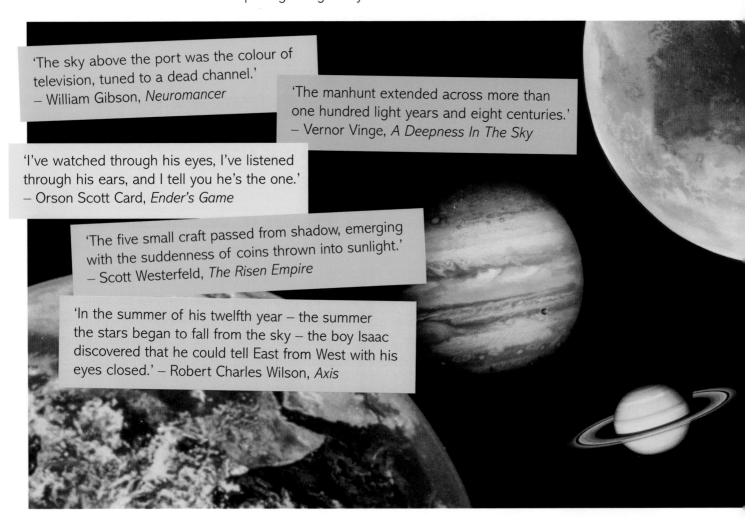

'The sky above the port was the colour of television, tuned to a dead channel.'
– William Gibson, *Neuromancer*

'The manhunt extended across more than one hundred light years and eight centuries.'
– Vernor Vinge, *A Deepness In The Sky*

'I've watched through his eyes, I've listened through his ears, and I tell you he's the one.'
– Orson Scott Card, *Ender's Game*

'The five small craft passed from shadow, emerging with the suddenness of coins thrown into sunlight.'
– Scott Westerfeld, *The Risen Empire*

'In the summer of his twelfth year – the summer the stars began to fall from the sky – the boy Isaac discovered that he could tell East from West with his eyes closed.' – Robert Charles Wilson, *Axis*

1 Which of the openings uses the most descriptive language?

2 Which uses the least descriptive language?

3 Which feels most as if it is describing a different world?

4 Which sentence most makes you want to continue reading the story?

Building your skills

1 Practise creating your own opening scene for a science fiction story. Imagine a kitchen in which a teenager is about to have breakfast. Suddenly, something unexpected happens – this could be a sudden newsflash on the TV or the teenager's realization that they have a special power, for example. Write the first paragraph of your story.

2 When you have finished your paragraph, swap it with a partner. Read your partner's opening and give them feedback on:

   a one thing you liked about it

   b one way they could improve their opening.

Developing your writing

Science fiction stories are often based on 'What if?' questions. They explore what life would be like if conditions were different. Choose one of the following 'What if?' questions; then think of a character and setting and write a 200-word story.

● What if scientists eliminated the ageing process?
● What if wars could be entirely fought by machines and didn't need humans?
● What if we could make robot pets?
● What if the world's computers all crashed at once?

Hints for Success

● Choose your storyline and then kick-start your story by creating a picture of a person in a place, only hinting that something is about to happen.

● Remember to draw your reader into the story by helping them to visualize the scene clearly.

Word Booster

Try to use some of the following words and techniques to make your science fiction writing more interesting:

● Powerful verbs: avoid *is/was* – e.g. *The dark sun climbed the distant horizon.*

● Lots of nouns that create a detailed world: *cup, screen, steam, birdsong*

Writing Historical Fiction

Big Picture   Like science fiction, historical novels are written to show us a different world; however, instead of presenting the future, they show us the past. As a result, we can often gain a better understanding of a particular period in history from historical fiction.

Skills   ● Explore the features of historical fiction.

Getting started   1 Think about why people might read historical novels rather than factual history books. Look at the statements below and decide whether you agree or disagree with them.

    a Historical novels enable us to see into a world we don't know.

    b They are more interesting than factual books because they include characters and dialogue.

    c They are better for people who are weak readers.

The writer John Hatcher is a leading expert in the history of the Black Death – the plague that swept across Europe between 1348 and 1350. In his book *The Black Death* he uses an unusual style – writing some chapters as a historian and others as a novelist. Compare these two extracts.

Extract A

As far as it is possible to judge, the pestilence struck Walsham close to Easter Day, which this year fell on 12 April, was fading fast by early June, and had departed by late June. Not a single tenant death was reported at the Walsham manor court session of 6 March, but there were no fewer than 103 reported at the next session, which was held on 15 June.

Extract B

John began to feel unusually weak and listless one late afternoon while pulling up the first crop of weeds [...] He complained, with slightly slurred speech, of tiredness and an unusual tingling sensation in his painful arms and legs, and Agnes put him to bed, praying that it was simply a heavy cold [...] She feared that he had caught the pestilence and would soon die.

2 Which text contains more facts – A or B?

3 Write down the main differences you notice in the language of the two texts.

4 Which extract did you find more interesting and why?

Building your skills

Writers of historical fiction need to know a lot about history, but they use the techniques of novelists to bring the world of history alive. Here's an example written by a Year 9 student who was asked to write the opening of a story based in the American Wild West (in the late 19th century).

> It was still dark. John Rayskill would normally be asleep at this time of the morning, but the sound of horses moving about had woken him. His eyes blinked open in the darkness. He listened. 'That's the one. Get it and bring it over here.' It was a voice he didn't recognize. His only thought was for the horses. Still listening, he hauled himself down from the wagon.

1 What historical details tell you that the story is set in the past?

2 What techniques does the writer use that you would expect to find in a novel?

3 How would you advise the student to improve his opening?

Developing your writing

Choose a period of history that you are interested in and practise writing the opening of a historical novel.

Think of:

- an invented or real-life character who you will build the story around
- details (clothes, furniture, scenery) which will help your reader to know where and when the story is set without saying it directly
- using different literary techniques to grab the reader's interest, for example, dialogue or descriptive language.

Hints for Success

- Read more historical fiction; this will help improve your writing.

- Don't be afraid to experiment with different words, phrases and viewpoints (e.g. from *I* to *he*).

Word Booster

Try to use some of the following words to make your historical fiction more interesting:

- Words that evoke a strong sense of place: *creaking, hazy, arid*

Writing Short Stories

Big Picture Short stories are not just novels with fewer pages; they require a different approach altogether in terms of structure. Among other ingredients unique to short stories, they need to be more concentrated and grab the reader's attention immediately.

Skills
- Understand the key features of short stories and practise writing a 50-word tale.

Getting started

Think of the day you have had so far today, starting with when you got up.

1 Try to tell the story of your day in just one sentence. Is it interesting?

2 If you were telling the same story in three sentences, what would you add?

Building your skills

If the only unique thing about short stories was that they were short, then they could be quite dull. They need to be short but fascinating. Here are some hints on how to achieve this:

> **Short story tips:**
> - Include one main character. The story should follow him or her.
> - Be brutal with your writing: reject every word or idea which doesn't improve your story.
> - Use a small amount of vivid description to help the reader to see, hear and smell the scene.
> - Have some conflict at the heart of the story – perhaps a feud, an unfulfilled dream or unrequited love.
> - Keep the reader guessing – don't give too much away.

1 Below is a short story. Before you read it:

  a Predict from the title, *The Trumpeter*, what you think will happen.

  b Pause after three sentences and, once again, predict what you think will happen.

2 After reading, describe in a sentence or two how you felt about the short story: what you enjoyed and what you didn't enjoy.

> **The Trumpeter**
>
> He was born with a long nose, big feet and protruding ears. His mother loved him. Intelligent, with retentive memory, he learned quickly. Instinct led him to become a trumpeter. He simply must. Was terrific. Afterwards he took over the herd and all the lady elephants thought he was wonderful.
>
> *M Gasecka*

Developing your writing

Choose one of the following tasks:

1 Write a 50-word story on a topic of your choice (think of a main character and then describe what happens to him or her one day).

2 Read the following 50-word short story and write it as a longer tale with more detail, practising building up to the surprise at the end. Try rewriting it as a story of 150 words.

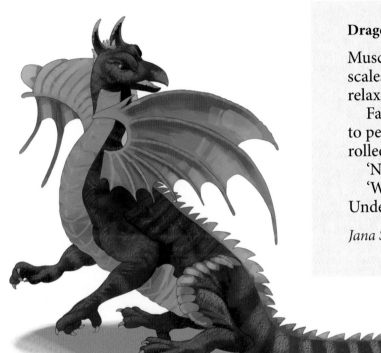

Dragon Tale

Muscles rippled under the blue-green scales as the dragon stretched, then relaxed.

Fascinated, I watched the creature freeze to perfect immobility. With a glare, he rolled down his sleeve.

'Nice tattoo,' I said, embarrassed.

'What tattoo?' he asked, turning away. Under his sleeve, I saw something move.

Jana Seely

Hints for Success

● Both tasks require a different kind of writing. The 50-word story needs extreme discipline, cutting out every unnecessary word and reducing the story to exactly 50 words.

● The second task requires more description. The aim here is to help the reader to visualize the scene more clearly. You could use description, dialogue and the inner thoughts of the character.

Word Booster

Try to use the following techniques to make your short story more interesting:

● Choose strong verbs, such as: *exploded, dropped, shuddered, stopped*

● Don't pile up adjectives and adverbs: they will waste words.

Making a Story More Interesting

Big Picture   Some people lack confidence when it comes to writing stories. They think that they have no interesting ideas or no story to tell. Often they struggle with getting ideas in the first place. This unit looks at how to find ideas and then develop them into an interesting story.

Skills
- Learn new techniques to make your stories more interesting.

Getting started

Reflect on how you approach writing stories. Look at the three topics below.
- The day the world changed forever
- Attack!
- The end of a friendship

1 Take a couple of minutes to consider which topic most interests you. Then write a brief outline of a story in bullet points.

Building your skills

1 How did you approach the task? What did you do? Did you decide on a topic straightaway? Did you feel stuck?

2 On a scale of 1 (not very) to 5 (very), how easy did you find coming up with an idea for your story?

3 Now look at these ten ideas for composition – for getting ideas in the first place:

   a Don't narrow down your ideas too quickly. Use a blank page and just let your brain respond to the titles. What images come into your mind? What names? What people and places?

   b Think of an emotion, for example, grief, pain, anger or hatred.

   c Think of a conflict and challenge: what might be the disagreement or frustration at the heart of the story?

   d Devise a character based on someone you know or someone you have seen in a film or read about in a book. Describe him or her.

   e Imagine a place. It can be a place you remember from experience or one you have made up. Draw it or use words to bring it to life.

   f Think of the character's perspective. Imagine looking through the eyes of your character. How does he or she feel? Why?

   g Write an opening sentence. This could focus on a detail of the setting or character or it could throw the reader into the story mid-action. Choose words that are as vivid as possible and that appeal to the senses.

   h Change a **proper noun** to a pronoun to keep the reader guessing (instead of 'Stephen didn't know where he was', write 'He didn't know where he was').

Glossary

proper noun: names of people, places or things, e.g. *Ravi*, *July*, *Rome*, *Prime Minister*; a proper noun always begins with a capital letter

i   Play around with point of view: try using the first person ('I didn't know where I was'), second person ('You didn't know where you were') or third person ('She didn't know where she was').

j   Experiment with tense in your opening sentence, moving the story to the present tense ('I don't know where I am') or past tense ('I didn't know where I was').

4   Now look back at the three topics in the 'Getting started' section. How might you have approached these topics differently, using the ten tips in this unit?

Developing your writing

Here are three story starting-points. Choose one and write a complete short story, or the opening section of a longer story, using some of the ten hints in this unit.

● Theme: Revenge
● Title: A Disaster Waiting to Happen
● Opening sentence: 'As she pulled the door closed, she knew that her life was about to change…'

Hints for Success

● Don't start trying to write straightaway. Use a blank page to scribble down ideas, pictures, characters and words.

● Use the ten hints in this unit to stimulate new ideas.

● Avoid predictable openings: *It was a really stormy day…* Make your writing more visual: *Storm clouds gathered above his head.*

Word Booster

Try to use some of the following words to make your writing more interesting:

● Sensuous adjectives: *gritty, smooth, perfumed, sour, bitter, ugly, bright*

Writing a Review (Part 1)

Big Picture   Reviewers give their opinion on something they have watched (like a film) or listened to (like a concert). A good review is designed to entertain as well as inform. This unit shows you how.

Skills   • Learn how to write a review that is both entertaining and informative.

Getting started

In newspapers and magazines, there are often pages devoted to reviewing new films, music, products and TV programmes.

1 Look at the description of four types of review below. Choose the one you are most likely to read and the one that you are least likely to read.

- Review of your favourite singer's concert
- Review of a new film you have been waiting to see
- Review of a TV programme on last night
- Review of a new mobile phone

2 For both of the reviews you have selected, suggest what the purpose of the review is and explain why you would or would not read it. The purpose of a review might be to persuade you to watch a film or buy a product, for example.

Building your skills

Read these online film reviews. Use the questions on page 91 to explore how each film review is designed to inform and also entertain the reader.

Journey 2: The Mysterious Island

Film: Action/Adventure ★ ★

More adventures for teen Jules Verne fan Sean (Josh Hutcherson) in this sequel to 2008's *Journey to the Centre of the Earth*. A distress signal leads Sean to the South Pacific in search of an uncharted island he believes inspired literary classics *Treasure Island*, *Gulliver's Travels* and *The Mysterious Island*: think tiny elephants, giant insects and gold-spewing volcanoes. Along for the ride is stepfather Hank (Dwayne Johnson), helicopter pilot Gabato (Luis Guzmán) and his daughter (Vanessa Hudgens), while the obligatory eccentric marooned adventurer is played by Michael Caine, no less.

It's a harmless family film with an old-fashioned spirit of adventure, but the writing doesn't live up to the promise of the premise.

Sherlock Holmes: A Game of Shadows

Film: Action/Adventure, Fantasy Period/Swashbucklers ★ ★

When Guy Ritchie's witty, enjoyable reboot of Sir Arthur Conan Doyle's iconic detective stories busted blocks back in 2009, a follow-up was unavoidable...

The best comparison to draw here is with the *Pirates of the Caribbean* sequels: the cast and crew remain unchanged, but a key ingredient is lacking. Perhaps it's a sense of spontaneity: where the first film seemed genuinely sprightly and off-the-cuff, the outcome of every thunderous, whizz-bang, CG-fuelled action scene in the sequel feels... inevitable.

The result is a fitfully amusing but largely unsurprising and uninvolving action-movie-by-numbers: elementary, and not in a good way.

1 Choose one of the reviews. What purely factual information does the reviewer give?

2 In the same review, what techniques does the writer use to show their opinion about the film?

3 Pick out two positive words or comments from each review.

4 Find two negative words or phrases in each review.

Developing your writing

Choose a film that you have seen recently and write a review of it, including:

- factual information about the film
- your opinion about the film
- what type of film it is
- a star rating.
- a summary of fewer than 50 words

Glossary

adjective: a describing word used to give more information about a noun, e.g. *The beautiful diamond sparkled magnificently.*

onomatopoeia: words which sound like the thing they describe, e.g. *splash*

verb: a word that tells you about the action in a sentence, e.g. *The fish swam around the tank.*

Hints for Success

- Remember your review should include both facts and opinions.
- Use an impersonal tone and vivid words to grab the reader's attention.

Word Booster

Try to use some of the following words and techniques in your review:

- Active **verbs**: *blasts, triumphs, busted*
- A range of **adjectives**: *enjoyable, gold-spewing*
- Literary devices, such as **onomatopoeia**: *whizz-bang*

Writing a Review (Part 2)

Big Picture Writing a Review (Part 1) got you thinking about why people write and read reviews, and how they use language and layout to present ideas. This unit helps you to explore your own style in writing a review.

Skills ● Write a restaurant review.

Getting started

Some reviews are designed to help readers make decisions. Based on reading them, we choose whether to see the film or buy the car, for example. This process is especially true of restaurant reviews.

1 Start by thinking about the essential ingredients in a restaurant review. Look at the list of elements below and rank them in order, starting with those that you think are most essential to a successful review.

A *An opening sentence that makes you want to read on*

B *Vivid descriptions of the place and food*

C *Factual information about price, location and type of food*

D *An insight into the writer's own character*

E *Personal language (using 'I' and 'me')*

F *Wordplay (like **puns**, jokes, **alliteration**)*

G *A recommendation about whether to eat there*

H *A star rating*

Building your skills

Here are the openings of two reviews about the same restaurant in London, written in different styles. Start by reading both:

R24 – great food and wine!

Lovely ambience – R24 has an intimate and cosy feel. The menu is quite limited but it does change daily. The food is wonderful. Service very polite and accommodating, kitchen was quick to get the food out. Only one problem: the plates were cold, which meant our veg was almost cold. Was very busy for a Wednesday night, so probably best to book. Overall, very enjoyable.

R24: meal for two, including drinks and service, £90

R24 is the restaurant equivalent of one of those people you know you should fancy, but can't – not quite. At the end of the date you say: 'The problem's not you, it's me', because you don't want to hurt their feelings when, of course, the problem is them: they have a really irritating laugh, or protruding nasal hair, or they don't know the name of the prime minister. And yet they are fabulous in every other way.

1 Use the word bank below to choose three words that you think best describes each review.

funny	cruel	detached	aggressive	friendly	warm
negative	honest	amateur	formal	informal	positive
trustworthy	easy-to-read	complicated	confusing	unfunny	sarcastic

2 Which text is:

a most informative
b most difficult to understand
c most enjoyable to read
d most negative?

Give reasons for your answers.

Developing your writing

Write a 150-word restaurant review. It can be about anywhere you have been out to eat or it could even be about your school canteen! Remember that your review should entertain as well as inform your reader.

Hints for Success

- Focus on description: describe what the place looks like, what the **atmosphere** is like and how the food looks.

- Keep practising your impersonal style: avoid using *I* and *me*.

- Try to use humour, if you like, so that your reader wants to keep reading.

Word Booster

Try to use some of the following words in your review:

- Positive adjectives: *memorable, sophisticated, charming*

- Negative adjectives: *uninspiring, disappointing, overpriced*

Writing Instructions

Big Picture Sometimes clear instructions can make a big difference to our lives. If someone gives us directions to a place, it causes a lot less stress if they are accurate; if we are using new equipment for the first time, we want instructions to be as simple to follow as possible. This unit will help you to write better instructions.

Skills ● Write instructions that are clear, accurate and concise.

Getting started

1 a How good are you at reading and listening to instructions? When did you last have to follow instructions? What was it for?

b What is the worst set of instructions you have ever been given?

c In your opinion, what is the most important ingredient in good instructions?

2 Read these badly written instructions, which tell you how to tie a tie.

Choosing the right tie to match your shirt is important, unless it's a school tie in which case you haven't really got much choice except whether to wear it properly tied up or (as is often more fashionable in many schools) halfway down your neck or with a massive great knot. Put the whole tie around your neck so that the thinner end is shorter than the longer end. Put the wider end over the thinner end and wrap it round twice before pulling the fatter end up through the loop by your neck and pulling it down through the knot that by now will have formed. Use the thinner and fatter end to pull the whole thing together.

a Why are these instructions so poor?

b If you were giving advice to the writer, what would you say? How would you advise them to make their meaning clearer?

Building your skills

Look at these instructions from a website, which explain how to make a paper helicopter.

Paper Helicopter Folding Instructions

1. Cut along all the solid lines on the diagram below.

2. Fold flap A forward and flap B to the back.

3. Fold flaps C and D both forward along the dotted lines.

4. Fold along the line E upwards to give a weight at the bottom.

5. You can scale up this model as much as you want. You just drop the model with the blades facing upwards and the weight at the bottom facing downwards for the best results.

FIG. 1

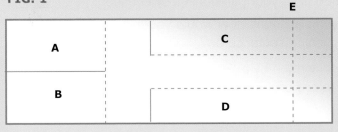

1 What do you like about this set of instructions? What makes them easy to follow?

2 Think of one way in which the instructions could be improved.

3 How do these instructions differ from those on page 94?

4 How has the writer structured the paper helicopter instructions?

Developing your writing

Choose one of the topics below and write a set of instructions. Use simple diagrams too, if you think it will help your reader.

- How to make the perfect cup of tea
- How to tie a shoelace

Glossary

connective: a word that links phrases or sentences together, e.g. *and, or, before, later*

imperative: command verbs, e.g. <u>*buy*</u> one today, <u>*stop*</u> that

Hints for Success

- Use a step-by-step logical approach; number the steps in sequence.

- Use short sentences.

- Use **imperative** verbs near the start of sentences (*cut, fold*).

- Use an impersonal style (avoid *I* and *me*). However, you may want to address the reader as *you*.

Word Booster

Try to use some of the following words in your instructions:

- **Connectives:** *first, next, then, now*

- Imperative verbs: *find, place, move, put*

Writing Personal Responses

Big Picture Quite often in English you are asked to write about something that happened to you personally. If you're not careful, this kind of writing can become quite boring. Here's how to keep your personal writing interesting.

Skills • Develop techniques to make your personal writing more interesting.

Getting started

Just because someone has an interesting topic to describe doesn't mean that it's going to be interesting for the reader. Imagine you are asked to write about a time when you were lost. You decide to write about a time when you got separated from your parents in a sweet shop.

1 If you were writing this account, how would you make it interesting? What would your opening sentence be?

2 Look at this example written by a Year 8 student. Write down one thing you like about this piece of writing.

> I was standing outside a shop. I was four years old. It was a sweet shop and it had lots of sweets that I was thinking would taste really good. Suddenly I put my hand into mum's hand and realized that it wasn't her hand at all. It was the hand of someone else. I looked around and couldn't find my mum and began to panic. Then I saw her.

3 Look at the statements below. Decide whether you agree, disagree or are unsure about them.

   a The words aren't interesting enough.

   b The style is a bit predictable.

   c It doesn't help the reader to visualize the scene.

   d The sentences could be joined by more interesting connectives.

   e The writer should have used some **questions** and **exclamations**.

   f The sentences are mostly too long.

4 Swap your answers with a partner. What did they think about the text?

Building your skills

Below are three suggestions for how to make your personal writing more interesting, plus examples of each technique.

Technique 1

Don't start personal writing with 'I was …' – it's predictable. Start by focusing on a detail or place. Try to start with an -ing or -ed verb; for example: 'Staring into the shop, I was spell-bound.'

Technique 2

Use verbs, adjectives and **adverbs** that help the reader to see, hear and smell the scene you describe: 'The window sparkled with shiny objects. Choking bus fumes filled the pavements.'

Technique 3

Try to vary sentences, using a question or exclamation occasionally, rather than another statement: 'I reached up for a familiar hand, but why did it suddenly feel different?'

1 Write the opening four sentences of a personal account describing a time when you were lost. Use the tips above to help you.

2 Swap your opening paragraph with a partner. Comment on two things you liked about their description and one area for improvement.

Developing your writing

Choose one of the topics below and, using what you have learned in this unit, write a piece of personal writing. Aim to write 150 words on one of the following topics:

- A place you love or hate
- A time you were disappointed
- A time you were in danger

Glossary

adverb: a word which gives more information about how an action is carried out, e.g. *The beautiful diamond sparkled magnificently.* Adverbs often end in -ly.

exclamation: a sudden cry or outburst expressing surprise or shock; ends with an exclamation mark, e.g. *The water was freezing!*

question: a sentence that asks for information or for a response and ends in a question mark, e.g. *Do you like ice cream?*

vocabulary: the range of words known by a person

Hints for Success

- You have a big **vocabulary**, so try to reject the first word that comes into your head and train your brain to test out alternatives.

- Keep focusing on the senses: help your reader to imagine what it was like to be where you were.

Word Booster

Try to use some of the following words in your personal writing:

- Words that evoke a strong sense of place: *calm, brittle, thunderous, menacing, lingering*

Writing a Formal Report

Big Picture The writing in a report needs to be clear and logical. Some reports are expected to be more formal than others and you need to know when to write in a personal tone and when to be more impersonal.

Skills
- Write a report that uses an impersonal voice.

Getting started

Scientific reports describe experiments. They usually require a style that is impersonal. They should focus on what happened rather than the person writing the report. This means:

- generally avoiding using 'I' or 'me'
- using more formal language (e.g. writing 'it is' rather than 'it's').

Read the following Science reports, both written by Year 9 students. How do they differ?

Text A

The investigation was planned to find out which type of antacid tablet is most effective. There are many on the market and our results could help customers to know which one to buy. We began by taking three types of tablet (Rennie, Tums and Settlers) and placed each in water, to which we added hydrochloric acid. We then measured the acid levels at the start and end of the process to see which tablet had been most effective in neutralizing the acid.

Text B

We wanted to see which kind of antacid tablet was best, but I wasn't sure what an antacid tablet was so I had to ask my friend, Kelly. Dr Geall, our teacher since September, gave us three tablets to test. I put each of the tablets into different beakers of water and watched them dissolve. The next thing was that we put methyl orange indicator in so that we could see what was happening. Then we put 50ml of hydrochloric acid in a measuring cylinder and put a bit of it into each beaker.

1 Which text do you think is better? Give reasons for your answer.

2 What two pieces of advice would you give to the student who has written text B?

Building your skills

1 Undertake a quick survey in a small group, or in your class as a whole, so that you have some data available to write up in a report. Choose one of the following topics for your survey and take a vote.

- How many students think that there should be more controls on the Internet in school? How many students disagree?
- What are the three all-time favourite films among students in your class?
- What is the favourite flavour of crisps among students in your class?

2 Jot down some notes that you want to include in your report. Make notes on the following:

- The aim of your report – what you wanted to find out
- The method of your survey – how you approached the task
- The results of your survey
- Any conclusions you drew from your survey

Developing your writing

Now write the full formal report. Include information about the aims, methods and results of your survey.

Glossary

contraction: a shortening of a word or words by dropping certain letters, e.g. the contracted form of *is not* is *isn't*; contractions are often used in informal speech and writing

synonym: a word with a similar meaning to another word, e.g. *large* and *bulky* are synonyms of *big*

Hints for Success

- Remember to keep your writing impersonal and formal: avoid using **contractions**, such as *isn't*, and try to find new ways of saying *I was...*

Word Booster

Try to use some of the following words to make your writing more formal:

- Interesting **synonyms**: *find out/discover/investigate*; *begin/start/commence/undertake*

- Analytical words: *analyse, investigate, explore, measure, suggest*

Writing a Semi-Personal Report

Big Picture
Writing a report means being clear and logical. You could be asked to write a report on anything from a sports match to a scientific experiment. This unit looks at reports which use a more semi-personal voice – not too chatty, but not too formal.

Skills
- Write a report using a semi-personal style.

Getting started
An informal report requires you to write about something that happened to you – such as an account of a holiday or experience.

1 Look at the list of possible assignments below:

> Write a report about a trip or visit taken with your school.

> Write a report of an investigation – for example, presenting the results of a survey recording students' attitudes to school uniform.

> Write a report about a process you have been involved in – for example, preparing for a school play or musical.

a Which of these should be the most personal in tone?

b Which assignment should be the most formal?

c Which report should contain the most information about you (the writer) and your own feelings?

d Which should not include any personal information at all?

Building your skills
Read the opening of this report written by a student in Year 7 who went on a school trip to Germany:

> The journey was OK which was good because I was really dreading it. We went by coach and had to leave really early in the morning. I was sitting next to Saif which was OK. We could get off the coach for the ferry crossing at Harwich. It was pretty choppy at sea and lots of people felt ill but I was fine and basically just spent the time chatting to mates. It took us another six hours after we had landed in Holland before we arrived in Germany; my first impression was how rainy it was.

1 Do you agree or disagree with the following statements about the report on page 100?

   a The writer gets the balance right between describing himself and describing what happens.

   b The vocabulary is interesting.

   c The writer paints a picture of the scene.

   d We get to know the writer better in this text.

   e The writing is easy to understand.

   f The writer uses a range of interesting sentences and sentence structures.

2 If you were advising the student to change three words of his report, which would they be? Why? What would you suggest he changes them to?

Developing your writing

Choose a visit or trip you have been on – it could even be your journey to school today. Write a report which entertains the reader as well as informs them about your journey.

Hints for Success

- Choose words which help the reader to see, hear or feel the scene.

- Use connectives which link ideas in sequence.

- If you are writing a longer piece, use subheadings to structure your report.

Word Booster

Try to use some of the following words in your report:

- Connectives for chronology: *first, later, next, as a result, earlier*

- Vivid verbs, adjectives and adverbs: *brake, turn, screech, halt, humid, worryingly*

Writing a Biography

Big Picture Writing a biography doesn't simply mean writing a whole book about another person. There are dictionaries of biography which contain written portraits of people through history, while magazines and newspapers will often include profiles of celebrities. This unit shows you how to write a biography.

Skills ● Structure and write an interesting biography.

Getting started Read the following extracts from some biographical writing about the footballer David Beckham.

Text A

David Robert Joseph Beckham OBE (born May 2, 1975) is an English footballer who plays for LA Galaxy. Named a member of Pelé's FIFA 100, he is one of the most famous players in the world, and considered a celebrity even outside the football world.

Text B

Famous, beautiful and very, very rich, David Beckham has travelled easefully from global celebrity to national icon. Like the Queen, there have been moments when his public lost faith. There were the dog days after his sending-off in the 1998 World Cup, his public spats with Alex Ferguson, the times when he was lost behind the sarongs, ponytails and tattoos.

Text C

He may be a multi-millionaire – but David Beckham proves he hasn't joined the upper crust as he tucks into a plate of pie and mash. Becks, 36, posed for a picture with a plate of the traditional East End grub after a visit to his favourite snack spot.

1 Which text is:

   a most informal   **b** most factual   **c** most interesting?

   Give reasons for your answers.

2 Which text gives you the strongest impression of what David Beckham is actually like?

3 Where do you think you would find each of the texts – for example, in a magazine, newspaper, website or encyclopaedia?

Building your skills

The three extracts on page 102 show that there are lots of approaches to writing about another person: some factual and impersonal; others informal and even funny.

1 Later, you will write a 250-word biography about someone from your family. Start by gathering facts and information, either from your existing knowledge or by interviewing the person. Aim to find out details about their:

    a early days: where and when they were born; where they lived

    b interests and hobbies

    c **anecdotes**: interesting things that have happened to them.

2 Write the opening of your biography. Practise some different opening sentences using the techniques below.

> Open with an anecdote, as if writing a novel or short story: 'When she was just six years old Asha Benton was chased through a field of sheep…'

> Start with a visual detail to show what the person looks like: 'Asha's hair is tied back today. It is kept out of the way while she focuses on the book in front of her…'

> Begin with a fact: 'Asha Benton was born in 1972 in a tiny cottage, a couple of miles outside Brighton. It was drafty, crowded and full of spiders…'

3 Swap your favourite opening with a partner. What do you like about the technique your partner used?

Glossary

anecdote: a short and amusing, or interesting, story about a real incident or person

Developing your writing

Write the full 250-word biography about someone from your family. Once you have finished, write down two features of your biography that you are pleased with and one area for improvement.

Hints for Success

- Bring your subject to life with vivid details of people and places.

Word Booster

Try to use some of the following words in your biography:

- Interesting verbs: *reflects, describes, exudes, hopes*

- Sensuous adjectives: *glistening, untidy, wrinkled, smiling*

Writing a Formal Essay

Big Picture   In some subjects, you will be expected to write essays. An essay is a piece of writing that explores a topic or issue and gives an opinion about it. The style usually needs to be formal and impersonal.

Skills   ● Plan and write a well-organized essay.

Getting started

The first step in writing an essay is making sure you understand the question being asked. Look at the following essay question:

> Many people complain that young children are exposed to too much advertising. Do you agree?

1   Start by looking at the words used in the title. Use the title to generate some ideas about what you might include in your essay. Jot down some thoughts in response to the terms of the question:

   ● 'Many people complain': Do you think that's right? Who might these people be?
   ● 'Young children': What age might this mean? What kinds of programme do they watch?
   ● 'Too much advertising': What does 'advertising' mean here? Do you know what rules already exist about advertising during children's programming?
   ● 'Do you agree?' Do you? Often the best essays partly agree or disagree with a point but also consider the alternative views.

Building your skills

Now start to build your essay structure.

1   Create a two-column grid, which includes a list of arguments for and against the statement.

2   Decide which are the more important points in each column and the least important points. In most essays (and in debating) you will want to put your main points at the start and give them the most emphasis. So, to organize your argument, put a '1' next to the most important point in each column, a '2' against the next most important point, and so on.

The style you use in an essay should be formal. Here's an essay which answers the question but is too informal. Read it and decide what the writer should do to get the tone right.

> I definitely agree that there is too much advertising on kids' TV. It makes them pester their parents all the time and, anyway, loads of the TV shows they watch are full of cartoon characters and fluffy creatures that are being sold in shops, so the last thing they need is even more marketing in the breaks.

3 How could the writer improve their response?

   a Identify two words she could change.

   b How could she improve her sentence structure?

   c How could she express and support her ideas more effectively?

Developing your writing

Write your response to the essay question in this unit. Alternatively, write a response to one of the following questions:

- Teachers should be paid by the results their students achieve. Do you agree?
- Spending money on research in space is a waste of resources. We would be better spending the money on our planet. Do you agree?

Make sure that you structure your argument carefully and you consider alternative views.

Hints for Success

- Take each main point in your argument and think of some examples to support it. The more you use specific examples, the stronger your argument will be.

- Remember to use an impersonal and formal style. Try to avoid using *I* and *me* too much until your final paragraph.

Word Booster

Try to use some of the following words in your essay:

- Vocabulary that analyses and persuades: *consider, suggest, analyse, could be argued*

- Connectives to link ideas and offer alternative points of view: *on the other hand, therefore, however*

Building an Argument in an Essay

Big Picture   One of the hardest parts of writing an essay is keeping your argument going and knowing what to say next. In an essay with an argument at its heart, you need to know how to develop your ideas logically.

Skills   ● Understand how to build an argument, setting out your ideas clearly.

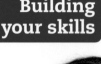

1 Do you have strong views about certain topics? Read the following topics and rank them in order, starting with those you most strongly agree with.

> **A** Breaking rules is sometimes justified.
>
> **B** We learn more out of school than in school.
>
> **C** Children should not be allowed to use the Internet unsupervised.
>
> **D** Animals should have the same rights as humans.
>
> **E** Humans aren't as important on the planet as they think they are.
>
> **F** Telling lies is sometimes necessary.

2 Compare your responses with a partner. How did your ranking differ?

Building your skills

1 It can be difficult to know what to say when building an argument. Look at the example question below.

> In schools, students are not really taught the subjects that will help them most in life. Do you agree?

Try to come up with as many ideas for the essay as you can, including:

● subjects that you think people need in life
● the subjects people study in your school
● subjects that may not be directly useful but can help with developing other skills, for example teamwork, critical thinking and creativity.

2 Once you have thought about the points, organize them into two lists – arguments for the statement and arguments against. Rank these arguments from most to least important for your essay.

Look at this possible structure for building an argument in this essay:

> **Paragraph 1:** Introduction – set out what you think the idea of school is and what different groups of people might think, but do not give your own opinion.
>
> **Paragraph 2:** Write about the most convincing argument in support of the statement.
>
> **Paragraph 3:** Write about the next argument that supports the statement.
>
> **Paragraphs 4 and 5:** Bring in ideas which oppose the viewpoint in the essay question. Use connectives that show that you are using contrasting opinions, for example: 'Some people, *on the other hand*, might argue that…'
>
> **Paragraph 6:** Conclusion – summarize the points and give your final opinion.

Developing your writing

Practise writing your essay in response to the question on page 106. Build your argument using the structure outlined above. Remember that the essay should show the different sides of the argument but you should conclude with your own opinion.

Glossary

personal pronoun: a pronoun that refers to a person, e.g. *I, you, me, they, us, we, her, him*

Hints for Success

- Try to avoid using the **personal pronouns** *I* and *me* until the last paragraph.

- Add variety to your writing: use questions, quotations and statistics if you can.

Word Booster

Try to use some of the following words in your essay:

- Phrases that give ideas authority: *it might be argued that*, *some people have suggested*, *it may seem that*

- Connectives: *similarly*, *on the other hand*, *therefore*, *despite*

Writing a Newspaper Article (Opinion)

Big Picture Newspapers don't just contain news reports. They also provide analysis and commentary on the news, plus a range of other features from fashion to crosswords.

Skills
- Craft an opinion newspaper article that keeps readers engaged.

Getting started

Newspaper columnists often write about controversial topics in a way which entertains the reader. They often also try to provoke strong reactions.

Opinion articles need strong openings to grab the reader's attention and then make them want to keep reading. How do they do it?

1 Choose one of the topics below. Think of the most boring opening sentence you can. Write it down.

> Extreme sports, such as paragliding or free running, should be banned.

> Social network sites do more harm than good.

> We should be less tolerant of students in school whose behaviour disrupts others' learning.

2 Swap your 'boring' opening with a partner. Comment on why their opening is not exciting.

Building your skills

Here are three ways you could try to grab your reader's attention from the start of your opinion article:

Technique 1 Use a drop paragraph. This is where you hold back your main point by first grabbing the reader's attention with a story or description:

> It's 6:30 and the sun isn't yet quite up, but huddled against the chill North Sea a group of figures in thick wetsuits haul equipment from a car boot. No one is around to see them and what they're doing won't be clear till later. These are the early morning kite-surfers, here on weekends watching the tides and choosing the right moment to wade into the pounding waves.

Technique 2   Open with a quotation or comment.

> 'Of course my family think I'm mad. On some really wet days, even I think I'm mad.' Kevin Hird clasps his hands tighter round the plastic cup of tea that is warming him briefly before the 'madness' begins. Kevin is a kite-surfer.

Technique 3   Use a personal anecdote. There might be something in your own past – a personal story – which could lead in to the story.

> The only time I tried kite-surfing, I gave up when I couldn't get the wetsuit properly zipped up. That was the end of my experience of 'extreme sports' – madcap activities like hang-gliding and kite-surfing. Adults who are normally sensible go and do stupid things and expect us to admire their courage.

1 Using the three techniques above, rewrite your 'boring' opening in three different ways. Which technique do you think worked best for your opening and why?

Developing your writing

Write an article in which you express your views on one of the topics below. Use the techniques from this unit to make sure that you capture your reader's attention. Remember to add strong opinions to your writing and to keep it entertaining.

- Why people who drive big cars are just attention-seekers
- Why keeping pets is wrong
- Why school should be a thing of the past

> **Hints for Success**
>
> - Be creative: try out new ideas, but also be self-critical.
> - Remember that you're writing an opinion piece: you're expected to be controversial!
>
> **Word Booster**
>
> Try to use some of the following words in your opinion article:
>
> - A mixture of formal and informal vocabulary: *consider*, *reflect*, *bang on about*

Writing a Newspaper Article (News)

Big Picture News journalism needs to tell a factual story accurately and in a small number of words. A good news story will focus on the events, people and places; the writer's own voice will usually be hardly noticed.

Skills
- Write a news story that communicates clearly and accurately.

Getting started

Nowadays, we get news in a number of different ways. Imagine a major emergency has taken place at an airport. Think about how different news sources might communicate this news.

1 Copy the grid below. Decide whether the statements are true or false for each news source.

	TV REPORT	RADIO REPORT	NEWSPAPER	ONLINE NEWSPAPER	SOCIAL NETWORKING SITE
It will have up-to-date news.					
It will have reliable information.					
It will give a clear overall impression of what happened.					

2 Which news source would you turn to in order to find out what has happened?

3 Which news source would you be least likely to use to find out reliable information about an incident? Why?

Building your skills

Use the grid on page 111 to explore the five key features of a newspaper story and answer the questions in the last column.

> **Glossary**
>
> **emotive:** provokes strong feelings
>
> **topic sentence:** a sentence often used at the beginning of a piece of writing to summarize the whole story; should include information about the 5Ws (*who*, *where*, *what*, *why* and *when*)

FEATURE	EFFECT	EXAMPLE	QUESTION
Headlines — usually no more than seven words; often use **emotive** vocabulary	Makes the story eye-catching	London's Airport Chaos	**a** Which is the emotive word in the headline?
Topic sentences — these summarize the main points in a story by telling us the 5Ws (who, where, what, why and when)	Gives the reader lots of information, without wasting words	Emergency crews were put on red alert because of a security breach at two of London's major airports yesterday.	**b** Why do you think the information about when the event occurred comes at the end?
Interesting vocabulary — words which help add drama, e.g. 'bid', 'crash', 'crisis', 'gloom'	Makes the story more interesting	A major crisis was narrowly averted yesterday as emergency services braced themselves for the worst airport accident for decades.	**c** Write down two ways in which the writer creates drama in this sentence.
Comments from eyewitnesses, usually with labels (name, occupation, age)	Brings the news story to life	Passenger Omar Stockley, 34, said: 'I've never seen anything like it in my life.'	**d** What two labels are used to give information about Omar Stockley?
Short paragraphs, often just a sentence long	Keeps the reader's eye moving down the page	Security forces are keen to inform passengers that the airports are safe.	**e** Why do short paragraphs allow us to read more quickly?

Developing your writing

Write your own 150-word newspaper story based on the story outline below:

- A burglar broke into a house overnight while the owner was asleep.
- The burglar was scared off by the owner's pet, Raymondo the parrot, who said, 'Hello there!'
- Owner Margery Lovett said that she usually wishes the parrot would keep quiet but is proud of what he did.

Hints for Success

- Refer to the grid, so that you get the style of your article right.
- Remember to write in short paragraphs.

Word Booster

Try to use some of the following words and techniques in your article:

- Active verbs: *smashed*, *shrieked*, *ran*
- Puns in the headline

Writing a News Headline

Big Picture   There is a real skill in coming up with a news headline that is eye-catching, dramatic or funny and makes the reader want to read the whole story. It's not just about choosing a small number of words; those words need to connect well with the story itself.

Skills   ● Explore the purpose of news headlines and practise writing them.

Getting started

The purpose of a news headline is to make us want to read the story beneath it.

Look at these newspaper headlines from the past 100 years. Use these examples to decide what you think are the conventions or rules for writing newspaper headlines today.

> *TITANIC SINKS FOUR HOURS AFTER HITTING ICEBERG;*
> *866 RESCUED BY CARPATHIA, PROBABLY 1250 PERISH;*
> *ISMAY SAFE, MRS. ASTOR MAYBE, NOTED NAMES MISSING*

> **PREMIER SAYS 'PEACE FOR OUR TIME'**

> **MEN WALK ON MOON**
> *ASTRONAUTS LAND ON PLAIN:*
> *COLLECT ROCKS, PLANT FLAG*

> **'Obama's American Dream'**

Glossary

noun: a thing, name or place, e.g. *panda, teacher, book, Ravi, London*

present tense: verbs which show an action takes place in the present, e.g. *The hyena howls.*

telegraphic style: a style of writing that deletes some words to make the text more concentrated

1 From each headline, what do you think the story that followed it was about?

2 Which headlines most make you want to read on? Which ones least make you want to read on? Why?

3 Based on looking at these headlines, what do you think the conventions are today?

   a Where on the page should newspaper headlines be placed?

   b Should headlines be all upper case?

   c How many words do you think should be the maximum for a headline?

Building your skills

Here are five key features of newspaper headlines.

FEATURE	EXAMPLE
Headlines have a **telegraphic style**. This means that they cut out all unnecessary words.	'Fire Rages at Luxury Hotel' rather than 'A Fire Rages at a Luxury Hotel'
They are written in the **present tense**, even though the events they refer to happened in the past.	'Factory Explodes' rather than 'Factory Exploded'
They use **nouns** and active verbs which have a small number of letters.	Typical newspaper nouns include: 'bid', 'fury', 'crisis', 'shock' Verbs include: 'fights', 'rages', 'clashes'
They use emotive language.	Emotions include: anger, joy, conflict, confusion, worry, panic
They often use wordplay, such as alliteration or puns.	Alliteration: 'Cheerful Charlie'; Puns: 'New Bakery has Flour Power'

1 Look at these newspaper headlines.

The Big Freeze

Go-get-'em Granny Foils Raiders

TV Chef Leaves Sour Taste

a For each one, write down two language features that you notice.

b Which headline most makes you want to read the story that follows it?

Developing your writing

The Sun newspaper has produced some funny but clever front pages for famous historical events. Look at this mock front page from 1859, which leads with a story about Darwin's theory of evolution.

Look at the following events from the past and try to think of some funny headlines you might invent for each of them.

a 1455: the invention of the printing press

b 1666: the great fire of London

c 1926: Scotsman John Logie Baird invents the television

Hints for Success

- Writing good headlines is about practising and being prepared to reject the first idea that comes into your mind.

- Be playful with language – use puns and wordplay.

Word Booster

Try to use some of the following words in your instructions:

- Short, pithy words: *bid*, *crisis*

- Emotive language: *fury*, *joy*

Using Persuasive Language in Advertising

Big Picture We are surrounded by advertising. Advertising aims to catch our interest and, often, surprise us. In this unit, learn how to use language to persuade your reader to change their habits or to buy your product.

Skills ● Explore the language of advertising and practise using it effectively.

Getting started

A **slogan** is a short, memorable phrase used in advertising. Read these advertising slogans, which come from a range of products.

Bring on the thirst-quencher (7-Up)

Impossible is nothing (Adidas)

The ultimate driving machine (BMW)

Buy it. Sell it. Love it. (eBay)

I'd rather have a bowl of Coco Pops (Coco Pops)

The world's local bank (HSBC)

1 Which of the slogans have you heard or seen before? Make a list of them.

2 Advertising slogans have different ingredients. Look at the list below and, for each one, find an example from the slogans above.

   a Slogans use very short sentences.

   b They include wordplay that reminds us of a well-known phrase.

   c Slogans use words in a way which surprises us.

   d They use words to suggest that the product will make our life better.

   e They use imperatives.

3 Which slogan do you like most and which do you like least? For each one, say why.

> ### Glossary
>
> **audience:** the group of people who will read a text
>
> **comparative:** an adjective that compares the qualities of two or more nouns, e.g. *This car is faster*.
>
> **slogan:** a short, memorable phrase used in advertising
>
> **superlative:** an adjective or adverb used to show the superior quality of something, e.g. *This car is the fastest*.

Building your skills

The language of advertising includes:

- Adjectives: 'new', 'free', 'ultimate', 'vital', 'amazing', 'special', 'easy'.
- **Comparative** adjectives: 'faster', 'better', 'happier', 'brighter'.
- **Superlative** adjectives: 'fastest', 'best', 'happiest', 'brightest'.
- Adverbs: 'now', 'quickly', 'soon'.
- Questions: 'Why not start today?', 'Who says you can't be beautiful?'
- Imperatives: 'Pick one up today.' 'Go on – make that change.'

1 Try to find an example of each of the language features above from different print and online adverts.

2 Make a note of the adverts you used to find these features. Which advert was the most effective in your opinion? Give a reason for your answer.

Developing your writing

Imagine you work for an advertising agency and a client has come to you for a new print advertisement (newspaper or magazine). They want to make their porridge brand more fashionable to a younger **audience**. Read the email below, which describes what the client wants to achieve.

| From: | Sue Whyand, Head of Product Development |
| To: | |

Most porridge advertising and packaging looks very old-fashioned. We want ours to appeal to young people, to feel like the perfect way to start the day. The name of the porridge is 'Oat'. Please come up with a slogan and newspaper/magazine advert that will make 15–25-year-olds want to buy it.

Come up with some slogan ideas and a mock-up of what the advertisement might look like. The advert should contain 50–100 words overall and should aim to persuade the younger audience that porridge offers a good start to the day.

When your advert is complete, write a short paragraph which includes information about the language features that you used and why you used them.

Hints for Success

- Keep your audience in mind: what will motivate them to buy this new product?

Word Booster

Try to use some of the following words in your advert:

- Comparative adjectives: *healthier, more nutritious, warmer*
- Imperative verbs: *choose, serve, eat, switch*

Writing a Leaflet

Big Picture It's easy to think that leaflets are the same as other texts but with more pictures and a different layout. In fact, effective leaflets are about clear and informative use of language, as well as layout. This unit gives you more information about what to include in a leaflet.

Skills ● Write an effective leaflet.

Getting started

Leaflets usually have two purposes – to inform or to persuade. However, some may do both.

1 Copy the grid below. For each topic, decide whether you think the purpose of the leaflet is to inform, to persuade or a mixture of both.

TOPIC	PURPOSE
'Stop smoking' leaflet	
Places to visit in Wales	
Leaflet about stopping animal testing	
A guide to improving your handwriting	
A guide to the best skateboard parks in the UK	
Charity leaflet about deafness	

Building your skills

Leaflets will usually include some of the following design and language features:

Design:
- A bold and colourful heading that stands out
- Images to catch our attention
- Colour and fonts which add visual interest to the leaflet

Language:
- Questions to hook our attention: 'How much do you know about cycle safety?'
- Imperatives to offer advice: 'Think before you buy.'
- Short sentences and phrases as subheadings
- Bullet points to make the text quicker to read
- Direct address to the reader, using 'you'
- Emotive vocabulary, such as: 'worried', 'harmful', 'unsure', 'healthy'

1 Here are the front covers of two leaflets. For each one, make two comments about the layout and two comments about the language used.

2 Which leaflet do you think is best? Give reasons for your answer.

3 Choose the leaflet that you didn't think was the best and draft a better version, showing how you might use language and design features to improve it.

Developing your writing

Choose one of the topics below and, on a piece of A4 paper, design a leaflet to inform or persuade your reader. Choose one of the following:

● A guide to the best features of your school
● Advice about how to choose a new phone
● Information about what each of us could do to help limit global warming

Hints for Success

● Don't focus just on layout: use the tips on page 116 to get your language right.

● Think carefully about your audience: how can you best inform or persuade them?

Writing a Speech

Big Picture Speeches are made by many people: politicians, guest speakers in school and even students. A good speech should leave us feeling motivated, inspired or more knowledgeable. This unit looks at the techniques behind great speeches.

Skills • Use language effectively in a speech.

Getting started

One of the most famous speeches in recent years was President Obama's inauguration speech, which he gave when he became President of the United States in January 2009. Look at an extract below:

> Our nation is at war, against a far-reaching network of violence and hatred. Our economy is badly weakened, a consequence of greed and irresponsibility on the part of some, but also our collective failure to make hard choices and prepare the nation for a new age. Homes have been lost; jobs shed; businesses shuttered. Our health care is too costly; our schools fail too many; and each day brings further evidence that the ways we use energy strengthen our adversaries and threaten our planet.

1 Find an example of:

   a powerful, emotive words

   b repetition of sentence patterns in threes

   c use of personal pronouns to show that he identifies with the audience.

Building your skills

Now look at the President's conclusion:

> America: In the face of our common dangers, in this winter of our hardship, let us remember these timeless words. With hope and virtue, let us brave once more the icy currents, and endure what storms may come. Let it be said by our children's children that when we were tested, we refused to let this journey end, that we did not turn back nor did we falter; and with eyes fixed on the horizon […] we carried forth that great gift of freedom and delivered it safely to future generations.

1 Write down five language features that President Obama uses in the conclusion of his speech and comment on their effectiveness. You might focus on:

- use of emotive language
- the rule of three
- how he addresses the audience
- the images he creates in his listener's mind.

2 Now look at this opening of a speech written by a Year 8 student for a debate about homework.

> Homework is a bad idea. I have worked out that we go to school for more than 1800 hours a year every year. Surely this is enough for us to learn everything we need to know. Teachers are paid to teach us and that should be happening at school. I say: end homework now.

a Write down one thing that you think works well in the speech.

b Write down three things that you would suggest to improve it.

Developing your writing

Write your own speech arguing whether homework is useful or unnecessary. Write a speech which:

- persuades listeners to support your point of view
- uses a variety of language techniques (such as repetition, emotive words, etc).

Hints for Success

- Think carefully about your audience as you write your speech. How can you best convince them of your viewpoint?

- Open your speech with a strong statement that gives your viewpoint; then conclude your speech with a similar statement. (*My speech will explain why homework is unnecessary./Today I have clearly shown you that homework demands to be abolished.*)

Word Booster

Try to use some of the following words in your speech:

- Personal pronouns to connect with your audience: *we, us, ours, you*

- Emotive adjectives: *unnecessary, unfair, oppressive*

- Powerful images: *crushed by workload, imprisoned by homework, liberated by success*

Writing Advice Texts

Big Picture Advice texts come in all kinds of formats. When writing an advice text, you need to think carefully about your audience. You must consider how much they already know about the topic and how this will impact on your text. Find out how to write effective advice texts in this unit.

Skills
- Explore the style and tone needed for effective advice texts.

Getting started

Examples of advice texts include:
- leaflets (how to link your DVD player to the television)
- magazine articles (how to change your image)
- books (how to become more self-disciplined in your life)
- websites (where to find the best value phone offer).

1 Write down examples of advice texts that you have read or used recently.

2 Look at the topics below. Where might you look to get advice on each one?

   a Advice on buying a new bicycle

   b Information about how to look after a pet tarantula

   c Advice on keeping your teeth looking good

   d Advice on how to make the perfect chocolate cake

   e Information about how to get a higher grade in Maths

Building your skills

Read the following advice texts. Both texts are written on the technical subject of computer programming.

Text A

Learn C++ a little at a time. Begin with the basics: things like variables, operators, functions and flow control. Notice how C++ treats memory and also how constructors and destructors work. Be sure to put all your code in namespaces, right from the beginning.

Text B

C++ is a compiled language, an upward compatible superset of C and an (incompatible) predecessor to Java. C++ compiles C programs but adds object oriented (OO) features (classes, inheritance, polymorphism), templates (generic functions and classes) and formatted text I/O (istream, ostream).

1 **a** On a scale of 1 (low) to 5 (high), how technical are the words used in text A and text B?

  b On a scale of 1 (low) to 5 (high), how impersonal is the style of each text? Do you get a feeling about what the writer is like?

2 Who do you think the typical reader might be for each text? Give reasons for your answers.

Developing your writing

Take a subject that you are an expert in and that your parents or grandparents may struggle with – for example, uploading photos to a social networking site.

Write the opening of two advice texts which give information about the topic you have chosen. Aim the first text at a non-specialist audience, who are not familiar with the subject. Write the second text for a **specialist audience** – for example, readers of your age who know some information about the topic.

Glossary

specialist audience: an audience who have some knowledge of the subject

Hints for Success

- Think about your choice of words – about how technical they should be and whether you might need to explain what they mean.

- Make one text personal and the other more impersonal: demonstrate that you know the difference.

Word Booster

Try to use some of the following techniques in your advice texts:

- For more impersonal writing, avoid using *I* or *me*.

- For more personal writing, use contractions: *isn't, it's*.

Writing an Evaluation

Big Picture Evaluations are an important part of many school subjects, like Science. Evaluations are a form of writing that describe a process and assess how well you have achieved something. They need precise and analytical language.

Skills
- Understand how to write an effective evaluation.

Getting started

Here's an extract from an evaluation by a student who had to come up with some designs for a new children's toy. How successfully does he evaluate it?

> I'm pretty pleased with the design of the toy. It's there to help them get their hand-eye coordination better. Turning the handle makes the maze move about and the ball moves through the maze and it looks great as the ball moves along the different 'alleys' of the maze. I tried it on my sister and she really enjoyed it. So overall I think this is a good product and I am pleased with it.

1 Look at the following statements about the evaluation. Decide whether you agree or disagree with each of them.

   a The language is too personal.

   b The evaluation is informative.

   c It explains clearly what the product is.

   d The style is impersonal.

   e It would be better if the writer avoided contractions.

   f The writer uses words which help to evaluate the toy.

2 If you were the student's teacher, what two pieces of advice would you give him to improve his evaluation?

Glossary

modal verb: a verb that signals mood or attitude, e.g. *might, could, will*

passive voice: a writing technique that avoids emphasizing the agent/subject of the action, e.g. *The window was broken by the boy* (passive) rather than *The boy broke the window* (active).

Building your skills

1 Based on reading the sample text above, and on your own experience, draw a spider diagram which shows what you think are the six essential ingredients for a good evaluation.

Evaluations can be especially helpful to a reader when they present information visually, such as in a grid. Subheadings can also help to organize your evaluation. Look at the suggested evaluation structure below, with highlighted subheadings.

> **Aim:** What do you want to test or prove?
>
> **Hypothesis:** What do you predict the results will be?
>
> **Procedure:** How did you carry out the experiment?
>
> **Results:** Draw up a grid or graph to present your results.
>
> **Discussion:** How did you make sure that your experiment was accurate? What mistakes did you make? How could you improve the accuracy?
>
> **Conclusion:** Did you find out what you expected? What has the process taught you?

2 How similar is this format to the way you are encouraged to write evaluations in other subjects, such as Science, Technology and Geography?

Developing your writing

Undertake an experiment in your class, testing one of the following:
- The fastest time in which someone can tie a shoelace or tie
- The average short-term memory of people in your class; ask your classmates to look at one page of a dictionary and to memorize as many words as they can in one minute.

Once you have the results, write up your evaluation in a formal style, using the framework above.

Hints for Success

- Use scientific vocabulary and avoid contractions.

- Try using the **passive voice** (*The class was asked to…*).

Word Booster

Try to use some of the following words in your evaluation:

- Scientific vocabulary: *explore, investigate, predict, conclude*

- **Modal verbs** that help you to explore possibilities: *would, might, should, could*

Writing about Poetry

Big Picture   Many students struggle when asked to write about a poem. They worry first about whether they will understand the text and then feel uncertain about what they should say about it. The aim is to write confidently showing that you know what the poem is about and that you can comment effectively on the language. This unit gives you the skills you need to write about poetry.

Skills   ● Learn how to write about a poem.

Getting started

1 Read this poem, *Stopping by Woods on a Snowy Evening*, by the American poet, Robert Frost. Consider how the writer creates a wintry atmosphere in the poem.

As you read the poem, make brief notes on:

a what the poem is about

b the poet's use of language to create a wintry scene.

Stopping By Woods on a Snowy Evening

Whose woods these are I think I know.
His house is in the village though;
He will not see me stopping here
To watch his woods fill up with snow.

My little horse must think it queer
To stop without a farmhouse near
Between the woods and frozen lake
The darkest evening of the year.

He gives his harness bells a shake
To ask if there is some mistake.
The only other sound's the sweep
Of easy wind and downy flake.

The woods are lovely, dark and deep.
But I have promises to keep,
And miles to go before I sleep,
And miles to go before I sleep.

Robert Frost

Building your skills

Read through the following three student responses to this poem.

Imagine you were their teacher. Think about the feedback you would give to each student about *what* they have written in their response and *how* they have written it. Highlighted words and puncuation have been spelled or used incorrectly.

Response A

I have been reading the poem and the atmosphere created is very unique.

I like the way you have described the atmosphere, you have put in lots of detail which gives you an affect as if you were there.

The way you have described the woods as 'lovely, dark and deep' is very creative, its giving you a bad and good side to the forest. Its basically telling you its scary but at the same time it's not!

the way you describe the atmosphere as snowy with a frozen lake and the woods filled up with snow makes you feel like its winter straight away. The way you describe the sounds makes everything alot more realistic and alot more imaginitive. its makes it feel a little romantic in a way!

Response B

The poet creates an atmosphere by talking about the wood, it says that the wood is lovely, dark and deep.

This makes the wood sound creepy, but then again it doesn't as it says its lovely. The woods are apparently dark; this makes it feel like there are evil things in there like in the Harry potter films!

The poem is interesting and intriguing. It makes you feel as if you are really there! the poem actually makes me want to be there as the place sounds so calm and peaceful. When it talks about the snow and flakes falling thats when I want to be their even more!

When it says that the harness bells shake it makes it sound like a fairytale. its sounds like nothing bad ever happens there.

Response C

As soon as I started reading the text, I immediately noticed the 'wintry' words and language I realized there were many wintry words, like: snow, snowy and frozen.

It's quite a calm and somehow a slow poem. I also noticed the ryming pattern in the first, second and last line of each verse. I'm not too sure about the meaning of all of the words but I'm pretty sure about most of the words meanings.

This particular poem makes me feel as though I should run inside and jump infront of the fire and read a good Book. The deep detail makes me feel as though I'm actually their, because of the vivid picture in my head.

1 Copy the grid below and use it to compare the three student responses. Mark your answers on the grid with a tick.

	RESPONSE A	RESPONSE B	RESPONSE C
Which response gives the most information about the poem?			
Which response gives the least information about the poem?			
Which response is the most interesting to read?			
Which response is the least interesting to read?			
Which response has used the most accurate spelling and punctuation?			
Which response has used the least accurate spelling and punctuation?			

2 Choose one of the responses. Look at the highlighted spelling and punctuation errors in the text. Rewrite the incorrect words using correct spelling and punctuation.

3 Using the same student response, write your feedback about their work as if you were their teacher. Use the following sentence openers in your comments:

What I like about your response is…

You could improve your writing by…

It would be easier for the reader to follow if…

My main advice is…

Developing your writing

Now write your own response to the poem, based on the following question:

> How does the poet use language to create a wintry atmosphere in *Stopping by Woods on a Snowy Evening*?

Remember to bear in mind the advice that you have given to each student about their response to the poem!

Hints for Success

- Organize your writing so that it takes the reader through the poem step-by-step.

- Focus on the writer's use of language, quoting specific words in your response.

- Aim to write in a formal (*is not* rather than *isn't*) and impersonal style (avoid using *I* too often).

Comparing Texts

Big Picture Many students feel confident when writing about a single text but feel less certain when asked to compare two or more texts. This unit uses the poem you read in the previous unit and asks you to compare it with author Dylan Thomas's memory of snowy days in his childhood.

Skills • Understand how to write a comparison of two texts.

Getting started

Text A is a poem about winter. Text B is an extract from autobiographical writing by Dylan Thomas, about memories of snowy weather in his childhood.

1 Read the two texts and consider their similarities and their differences. As you read, make notes on:

   a similarities and differences in the content of the texts (i.e. what they are about)

   b similarities and differences in how the texts are written and the language used (e.g. the words they choose, whether the text is formal/informal, serious/comic, personal/impersonal, easy to understand/difficult).

Text A

Stopping By Woods on a Snowy Evening

Whose woods these are I think I know.
His house is in the village though;
He will not see me stopping here
To watch his woods fill up with snow.

My little horse must think it queer
To stop without a farmhouse near
Between the woods and frozen lake
The darkest evening of the year.

He gives his harness bells a shake
To ask if there is some mistake.
The only other sound's the sweep
Of easy wind and downy flake.

The woods are lovely, dark and deep.
But I have promises to keep,
And miles to go before I sleep,
And miles to go before I sleep.

Robert Frost

Text B

Years and years ago, when I was a boy, when there were wolves in Wales, and birds the colour of red-flannel petticoats whisked past the harp-shaped hills, when we sang and wallowed all night and day in caves that smelt like Sunday afternoons in damp front farmhouse parlors, and we chased, with the jawbones of deacons, the English and the bears, before the motor car, before the wheel, before the duchess-faced horse, when we rode the daft and happy hills bareback, it snowed and it snowed. But here a small boy says: 'It snowed last year, too. I made a snowman and my brother knocked it down and I knocked my brother down and then we had tea.'

'But that was not the same snow,' I say. 'Our snow was not only shaken from white wash buckets down the sky, it came shawling out of the ground and swam and drifted out of the arms and hands and bodies of the trees; snow grew overnight on the roofs of the houses like a pure and grandfather moss, minutely ivied the walls and settled on the postman, opening the gate, like a dumb, numb thunder-storm of white, torn… cards.'

Building your skills

Read through the following three student responses. All three responses compare texts A and B. Highlighted words and punctuation have been spelled or used incorrectly.

Response A

Both pieces of writing have snow falling at one point. Both of them have horses at one point in the story. The poem is different to the text because the text has a little background and the poem dosen't. The text explains alot more about the setting of were the text is set and the poem just goes straight in to the actual poem. The text is a lot more detailed. the language in the poem is abit harder to understand because it's older. The language in the text is a bit more modern than the poem. I would say the poem was written before text B. The text and the poem are quite simillar as they both explain the same kind of thing. The peom talks about the atmosphere a lot less than the text.

Response B

The texts are the same because they are both about snow. Text A rhyms and is about a snowy forest or a forest filling up with snow and a man stopping there with his horse and thinking the farmer wont mind. Text B is about a boys memories. He is talking about when he was younger and playing in the snow with his brother.

The poem A has a lot of description about the atmosphere and has a lot of descriptive words. It sets the sceen really well.

The difference between the two texts is text B seems more like a story than a poem because it does not rhyme and has speech. One simelarity is that both poems are written in the first person.

Response C

The two texts are both about the snow and the beauty of it. The language both writers have used, is descriptive as they describe the snow and its surroundings. They make you feel in the mood for winter and this makes you appriciate it. You would read text A quiet slowly because there is a lot of information aswell as describing lots of things at once. Also this makes you feel cold like it really is winter. As soon as I started reading these descriptive poems I wanted to read even more because they is so detailed.

1 Copy the grid below and use it to compare the three student responses. Mark your answers on the grid with a tick.

	RESPONSE A	RESPONSE B	RESPONSE C
Which response gives the most information about the texts?			
Which response gives the least information about the texts?			
Which response is the most interesting comparison?			
Which response is the least interesting comparison?			
Which response has used the most accurate spelling and punctuation?			
Which response has used the least accurate spelling and punctuation?			

2 Choose one of the responses. Look at the highlighted spelling and punctuation errors in the text. Rewrite the incorrect words using correct spelling and punctuation.

3 Using the same student response, write some feedback about their work as if you were their teacher. Use the following sentence openers in your comments:

> What I like about your comparison is…

> I think your choice of words…

> Your comparison would be better if…

> To improve your writing you could…

Developing your writing

Now write your own comparison of the two texts, based on the following question:

> What similarities and differences do you notice between texts A and B? How have the writers used language to describe the scene in both texts?

Aim to write at least 150 words. Use the following structure in your comparison:

- Write a paragraph that explains what the texts are about, highlighting any similarities and differences.
- Write a paragraph about the settings of each text, noting similarities and differences.
- Write about the writers' use of vocabulary in text A and text B. Remember to comment on what is similar and what is different.

Hints for Success

- Aim to write in a formal and impersonal style (avoid using *I* too often).

- Try to link the texts using connectives, such as: *similarly, on the other hand, unlike the first text, in a similar way, in contrast.*

Writing about a Non-Fiction Text

Big Picture Lots of students feel more confident when writing about stories and poems than about non-fiction texts, such as leaflets and newspaper articles. Yet you just need to apply the same reading skills that you use when reading a fiction text as for non-fiction texts.

Skills • Learn how to write a response to a non-fiction text.

Getting started Students from a Year 9 class were given a website to look at and then to comment on. This was designed to test their reading and writing skills.

1 Look at the website below.

   a Write a paragraph commenting on some of the design and language features of the text, including how it is laid out, who it might be aimed at and what it is designed to do.

   b Write a paragraph saying how you think the website could be improved – either in layout or language.

HOW TO...

Select a Gift for your Grandmother

Grandmas are just like Grandpas, in that they can hardly ever think of a thing they need. Being practical is a good idea, but splurging a little will always make Grandma happy.

Instructions

1. Ask her what she wants. This information can get you going in the right direction and can save guesswork.

2. Buy her a prepaid phone card so that she can talk to the grandkids without running up her phone bill.

3. Give her a gift certificate for hair styling, a manicure or a pedicure.

4. Fill a gift basket with her favourite 'splurge' foods or beauty products.

5. Subscribe to a magazine or buy a book she would enjoy. Get large print editions if needed.

6. Make a book about her life. Include photos, news clippings and letters from friends.

7. Have a formal family picture taken and put it in a nice frame.

8. Buy her something for the yard, or hire someone to take care of her yard.

9. Make something. Grandmas love homemade gifts from you or the kids.

10. Buy a year's membership to a local museum or another attraction she enjoys.

Things you'll need

Greeting cards

Gift baskets

Photograph in picture frames

Building your skills

Read through the following three student responses. All three responses look at how the website uses language and layout, and comment on how the website could be improved. Highlighted words and punctuation have been spelled or used incorrectly.

Response A

a) I think this website is very good because all the information is spaced out. I also think that the website is very formal which is good, because it shows that the websight is reliable and capable of supplying things. I think this website is aimed at people who are grandmothers and don't really use tecnology much.

b) I think that this website could be improved by having more pictures on there, because at the moment the website looks a bit boring. When a website looks boring people tend to click straight of it. Also the language used on the website is quite formal so I think it would be good to have a little bit of informal language, otherwise children wont go on the website.

Response B

a) I think this website has been set out clearly and neatly, with numbers at the side so that you can follow what your doing or see what your doing next. There are different things you can look up and it is labled clearly! This maybe aimed at grandchildren helping themselves get the best present for there grandmother for her birthday. The site is designed to make it easier for children to get there grandmother a present.

b) I think this website could be improved by having bigger font so that we can read it easier. It could have had more pictures to make children want to read it. It would also make it a bit more colourful and intresting. The thing I most like about this website are the instructions. They are easy to read because of the step-by-step points. I quite like the way it is laid out, you can see where everything is and it's clear to read.

Response C

a) The website is not very interesting and it needs more images to make it more interesting because at the moment it is quite boring. It has quiet a lot of information but this is not really very interesting. The colour scheme isnt much interest and could be done better.

b) I would improve the website by changing the colours to something more eye-catching like red and making it more exciting with more interesting words. I don't think it really get's you wanting to read it in much detail at the moment.

1 Copy the grid below and use it to compare the three student responses. Mark your answers on the grid with a tick.

	RESPONSE A	RESPONSE B	RESPONSE C
Which response gives the best analysis of the website?			
Which response gives the worst analysis of the website?			
Which response has used the most accurate spelling and punctuation?			
Which response has used the least accurate spelling and punctuation?			

2 Choose one of the responses. Look at the highlighted spelling and punctuation errors in the text. Rewrite the incorrect words using correct spelling and punctuation.

3 Using the same student response, write some feedback about their work as if you were their teacher. Use the following sentence openers in your comments:

I really liked…

You seemed to…

Your responses were…

Your use of language was…

You could improve your writing by…

Developing your writing

Now write your own analysis of the website, based on the following question:

> Look at the website 'How to Select a Gift for your Grandmother'.
>
> **a** How is language, layout and design used in the website to attract readers? Who do you think the website is aimed at?
>
> **b** How do you think the website could be improved?

Aim to write two paragraphs.

Hints for Success

- Write in a formal way (*is not* rather than *isn't*).
- Aim to comment on the language of the text.
- Use short and long sentences to make your writing varied.

Writer's Toolkit

Common errors   This is a quick reference guide to help you to learn about easily confused words and phrases.

A
- Affect/Effect:
    - Affect is a verb, e.g. *He was genuinely affected by the music*.
    - Effect is a noun, e.g. *His arrival had a big effect*.
- All right, not 'alright'
- All sorts, not 'allsorts'
- A lot, not 'alot'

B
- Basically – this word is unnecessary in most writing

C
- Continuous/Continual:
    - A continuous noise is one which never stops.
    - A continual noise is one which is frequent but with interruptions.
- Comprise or consists of but not 'comprises of'

D
- Dependant/Dependent:
    - Dependant is a noun, e.g. *He looked after his dependants*.
    - Dependent is an adjective, e.g. *They were dependent upon him*.
- Different from, not 'different than'
- Discreet/Discrete:
    - Discreet means 'modest' or 'restrained'
    - Discrete means 'separate'
- Disinterested/Uninterested:
    - Disinterested means 'neutral' or 'objective'
    - Uninterested means 'not interested'

E
- Everyday/Every day:
    - Everyday is an adjective, e.g. *an everyday remark*.
    - Every day is a noun and adverb, e.g. *it happens every day*.

F
- Formally/Formerly:
    - Formally means 'in a formal way'
    - Formerly means 'in the past'

I
- Imply/Infer:
    - Imply means to express something indirectly, e.g. *She implied that his idea was ridiculous*.
    - Infer means to draw conclusion(s) from what has been indirectly expressed, e.g. *He inferred that she thought he was crazy*.
- It's/Its:
    - It's means *it is* or *it has*
    - Its is possessive, e.g. *The cat played with its toy*.

L

- Like – use *as if* in place of *like*, e.g. *It looks as if he will be late*.
- Led/Lead:
  - Led is the past tense of *to lead*.
  - Lead is a rope for a dog or a metal.
- Less/Fewer:
  - Less is used for quantities that cannot be counted, e.g. *There is less water in the bottle now*.
  - Fewer is used for items that can be individually counted, e.g. *fewer than ten bottles*.
- Literally – use with care: not *He literally jumped out of his skin* (although it may be used in informal contexts to add emphasis)

M

- Meet – not 'meet with'
- Momentarily – *he stopped momentarily*, not the Americanism *I'll be there momentarily*
- More than – it's better to use 'more than' than 'over', e.g. *It cost more than £27*.

N

- No one, not 'no-one'

O

- On to, not 'onto'
- Outside, not 'outside of'

P

- Practice/Practise:
  - Practice is a noun, e.g. *I have football practice*.
  - Practise is a verb, e.g. *I need to practise*.
- Principal/Principle:
  - Principal means 'head of a school'
  - Principle means 'belief'
- Program/Programme:
  - Program means 'something which runs on a computer'
  - Programme means 'something we watch on television or buy at a theatre'

T

- Theirs (no apostrophe)
- Try to, not 'try and'

U

- Under way, not 'underway'
- Until, not 'up until'

W

- While, not 'whilst'

Y

- Yours (no apostrophe)

Tricky spellings

Here is a list of tricky spellings. Pay careful attention to the letters that are underlined – these sections are often where students make mistakes!

A
accident<u>all</u>y
a<u>cc</u>o<u>mm</u>odation
all sorts (not 'allsorts')
a lot (not 'a lot')
ar<u>gum</u>ent

B
be<u>au</u>tiful
bel<u>ie</u>ve

C
cal<u>e</u>nda<u>r</u>
cat<u>e</u>gory
chang<u>e</u>able
co<u>mm</u>i<u>tt</u>ed
con<u>sci</u>ence

D
defi<u>nite</u>ly
di<u>sci</u>pline

E
emba<u>rr</u>assment
equi<u>p</u>ment
exist<u>e</u>nce
experi<u>e</u>nce

F
Feb<u>r</u>uary
for<u>ei</u>gn

G
gr<u>ate</u>ful
gu<u>ara</u>ntee

H
h<u>ei</u>ght
hum<u>o</u>rous

I
immedia<u>te</u>ly
inde<u>pen</u>dent
indispens<u>able</u>
its (possessive: *the cat licked its tail*)
it's (contraction: *it's beginning to rain*)

J
jud<u>ge</u>ment

L
l<u>ei</u>sure
l<u>ia</u>ison
lib<u>r</u>ary

M
maint<u>e</u>nance
mini<u>a</u>ture
mischiev<u>ous</u>

N
ne<u>cess</u>ary
notic<u>e</u>able

O
occa<u>s</u>ionally
o<u>cc</u>u<u>rr</u>ence

P
pers<u>eve</u>rance
po<u>sse</u>ssion
princip<u>al</u> (headteacher/main idea)
princip<u>le</u> (belief)
privil<u>e</u>ge
pro<u>nun</u>ciation
public<u>ly</u>

Q
questio<u>nn</u>aire
<u>queue</u>

R
rec<u>ei</u>ve
reco<u>mm</u>end
refe<u>rr</u>ed
rel<u>ev</u>ant
<u>rhy</u>me
<u>rhy</u>thm

S
sent<u>e</u>nce
se<u>para</u>te

T
th<u>eir</u> (possessive)
th<u>ere</u> (place)
they<u>'re</u> (contraction of 'they are')

U
unti<u>l</u>

V
vac<u>uu</u>m

W
w<u>ea</u>ther
w<u>h</u>ether
w<u>ei</u>rd

Words that sound the same but are spelt differently (homophones):

1. seen, scene
2. hear, here
3. their, there, they're
4. ate, eight
5. wheel, we'll
6. new, knew
7. wear, where
8. it's, its

Words with silent letters:

1. know, knee, knife, knit, knuckle
2. should, could, would
3. aisle, island
4. wrap, wrinkle, write, wrist
5. debt, doubt
6. listen, soften, castle, often
7. February
8. Government

Connectives checklist

Connectives are words that link phrases or sentences together, such as 'and', 'or, 'before' and 'later'. Look at the grid below to see how you can use connectives in your writing.

PURPOSE	EXAMPLES
Adding information	and also as well as moreover in addition
Explaining cause and effect	because so therefore thus consequently
Comparing information	equally similarly in the same way likewise as with
Contrasting information	whereas alternatively instead of otherwise unlike on the other hand
Emphasizing information	above all in particular especially significantly indeed notably obviously clearly
Illustrating a point	for example such as for instance as revealed by in the case of
Qualifying information	however although unless except apart from despite
Sequencing information	next then first, second finally meanwhile after

My writing   This page is designed to help you to track your own progress. Copy out the grids below and use them through the year to note the areas you need to work on. Try to include any strategies or solutions that you have learned to help you correct your common errors and misspellings.

MY COMMON ERRORS	MY STRATEGIES/SOLUTIONS
This might include: • forgetting capital letters • using commas instead of full stops.	This might include: • ways of helping yourself to correct your errors • any notes.

MY TRICKY SPELLINGS	MY STRATEGIES/SOLUTIONS
Note down words that you have struggled to spell correctly.	Think about visual clues, sound clues and memory clues that could help with your spelling.

MY CONNECTIVES	IMPACT
Note down new connectives that you have begun to use in your writing.	Write down how your writing has improved as a result.

Glossary

active voice: a writing technique where the subject of the sentence performs the action; e.g. *He announced the news* (active) rather than *The news was announced by him* (passive).

adjective: a describing word used to give more information about a noun, e.g. *The beautiful diamond sparkled magnificently.*

adverb: a word which gives more information about how an action is carried out, e.g. *The beautiful diamond sparkled magnificently.* Adverbs often end in -ly.

adverbial: a group of words which act like an adverb in a sentence, describing how or when something happened, e.g. *Before the play…*

agent: the person or thing that performs the action described by a verb, e.g. *the snow* is the agent in the following sentences: *The snow fell heavily that night* and *Her path was covered by the snow;* the agent is also known as the **subject**

alliteration: repetition of the first sound in two or more words or phrases, e.g. *the wild winds of winter*

anecdote: a short and amusing, or interesting, story about a real incident or person

atmosphere: tone or mood

audience: the group of people who will read a text

character: a person (and sometimes an animal) presented in a novel, play or film

chronological: in the order in which the events happened, starting with the earliest event

clause: a group of words which includes a subject and a verb, e.g. *When I run in the evening*

cliff-hanger: a suspenseful ending to a novel or film

cohesion: the way ideas are linked within a text

colloquial: informal words that would be used in conversation, e.g. saying *It's cool* when you mean something is good

colon: (:) a punctuation mark used before lists and quotations

comma: (,) a punctuation mark used to show a pause in a sentence and to separate items in a list, e.g. *I like computers, football, tennis and playing my guitar.*

comparative: an adjective that compares the qualities of two or more nouns, e.g. *This car is faster.*

complex sentence: a sentence containing a subordinate clause

compound sentence: a sentence that is made up of two main clauses joined by a conjunction, e.g. *I like pizza and I like pasta.*

conjunction: a word that links phrases or clauses together, also known as **connectives**

connective: a word that links phrases or sentences together, e.g. *and, or, before, later*

contraction: a shortening of a word or words by dropping certain letters, e.g. the contracted form of *is not* is *isn't*; contractions are often used in informal speech and writing

determiner: a word that comes before a noun to show how the noun is being used, e.g. *the, a, some*

dialect: a variety of language used in a particular location or by a particular group, e.g. American English

dialogue: speech in a novel, play or film

discourse marker: words or phrases used to signal a topic change or time-shift, e.g. *before, alternatively*

emotive: provokes strong feelings

exclamation: a sudden cry or outburst expressing surprise or shock; ends with an exclamation mark, e.g. *The water was freezing!*

exclamation mark: (!) a punctuation mark, used at the end of a sentence, to show shock

filler: words that are used in conversation to fill pauses, e.g. *er*, *um* and *y'know*

finite clause: a clause that contains a main verb and can stand on its own as a sentence

front-shifting: moving an element of a sentence to the front, in order to emphasize it, e.g. <u>*That car we saw*</u> *– there was something suspicious about it.*

full stop: (**.**) a punctuation mark used to mark the end of a sentence

genre: type of story, e.g. *horror, romance, crime fiction*

hypernym: the main word in a category, e.g. *traffic*

hyponym: specific examples within a category, e.g. *car* is a hyponym for *traffic*

idiolect: a person's personal speech habits and patterns, including the words they use and their accent

imperative: command verbs, e.g. <u>*buy*</u> *one today,* <u>*stop*</u> *that*

intonation: the rise and fall of a person's voice when speaking

metaphor: a literary device which compares two things by saying that one thing is another, e.g. *He was the apple of her eye.*

modal verb: a verb that signals mood or attitude, e.g. *might, could, will*

modify: add more detail or tell us more information, e.g. in *the fierce teacher* the noun *teacher* is modified by the adjective *fierce*; in *the car swerved suddenly* the verb *swerved* is modified by the adverb *suddenly*

non-finite clause: a clause that does not contain a main verb and cannot stand on its own as a sentence

noun: a thing, name or place, e.g. *panda, teacher, book, Ravi, London*

noun phrase: a noun made up of more than one word, e.g. *the elephant*

onomatopoeia: words which sound like the thing they describe, e.g. *splash*

passive voice: a writing technique that avoids emphasizing the agent/subject of the action, e.g. *The window was broken by the boy* (passive) rather than *The boy broke the window* (active).

past tense: verbs which show an action has taken place in the past, usually in the -ed form, e.g. *The hyena howled.*

personal pronoun: a pronoun that refers to a person, e.g. *I, you, me, they, us, we, her, him*

personification: a literary device which takes things that are not alive and describes them as if they are, e.g. *The wind scratched at the door.*

phrase: a group of two or more words that does not include a main verb

plot: events placed in a pattern to tell a story

polysyllabic: a word containing more than one syllable, e.g. *helicopter* contains four syllables: *hel-i-cop-ter*

post-modify: add description after a noun

pre-modify: add description before a noun

present tense: verbs which show an action takes place in the present, e.g. *The hyena howls.*

pronoun: a word that takes the place of a noun in a sentence, e.g. *it, that, he*

pronunciation: the way a word sounds when it is spoken

proper noun: names of people, places or things, e.g. *Ravi, July, Rome, Prime Minister*; a proper noun always begins with a capital letter

pun: a play on words; they sometimes play on words that sound alike but have different meanings or the different meanings of a word, e.g. *The oil well driller had a* <u>*boring*</u> *job.*

punctuation: signs used in written language to separate elements in sentences and to signal an attitude or relationship

question: a sentence that asks for information or for a response and ends in a question mark, e.g. *Do you like ice cream?*

question mark: (**?**) a punctuation mark, used at the end of a sentence, to show that a question is being asked

relative clause: groups of words that begin with a relative pronoun (*that, which, who, whose*), e.g. *The cake, which was delivered, arrived in time for the party.*

semi-colon: (**;**) a punctuation mark which can be used instead of a full stop to separate two sentences that are closely related to each other, or to separate items in a list

sentence: a unit of meaning that makes sense on its own; it begins with a capital letter and ends with a full stop, question mark, or exclamation mark, e.g. *The girl caught the ball.*

setting: location of a novel, play or film

simile: a literary device which compares two things, using the words *like* or *as*, e.g. *Her hair was golden like the sun.*

slang: informal words and phrases, which are often used in speech by a particular group of people

slogan: a short, memorable phrase used in advertising

specialist audience: an audience who have some knowledge of the subject

Standard English: the form of English that is considered the 'norm' and is typically used in formal situations

subject: the thing or person in a sentence which carries out the action, e.g. *fish* is the subject in the following sentence: *The fish swam around the tank.*

subordinate clause: a clause that does not make sense on its own, e.g. *When I run*

superlative: an adjective or adverb used to show the superior quality of something, e.g. *This car is the fastest.*

suspense: the way writers hold back information to keep readers guessing what will happen next; also known as **tension**

synonym: a word with a similar meaning to another word, e.g. *large* and *bulky* are synonyms of *big*

telegraphic style: a style of writing that deletes some words to make the text more concentrated

tension: the way writers hold back information to keep readers guessing what will happen next; also known as **suspense**

topic sentence: a sentence often used at the beginning of a piece of writing to summarize the whole story; should include information about the 5Ws (*who, where, what, why* and *when*)

verb: a word that tells you about the action in a sentence, e.g. *swam* is the verb in the following sentence: *The fish swam around the tank.*

viewpoint: the way a writer recounts a story, e.g. first person (*I…*), second person (*you…*) and third person (*she/he/they…*)

vocabulary: the range of words known by a person